Scorned
but Not Broken
a memoir

by

Tonya Ward-Blackshear

Scorned, but Not Broken

Copyright © 2016 Tonya Ward-Blackshear
All rights reserved.

Published by:
NyreePress Literary Group
Fort Worth, TX 76161
1-800-972-3864
contact@nyreepress.com
www.nyreepress.com

All rights reserved. No part of this book may be used or reproduced by any means, graphic, electronic, or mechanical, including photocopying, recording, taping or by any information storage retrieval system without the written permission of the publisher. Copying this book is both illegal and unethical.

ISBN 13: 978-1-945304-10-1
ISBN-10: 1-945304-10-3
Library of Congress Control Number: pending

Memoir / Autobiography

Printed in the United States of America

Acknowledgments

Lord, I am just an empty vessel and I ask that you fill me up and use me for your glory. My Heavenly Father who sits high and looks low, you are the author of this book and my life. You deserve all the glory, honor and praise for being a comforter to me in my lonely and sad days. You have been a mother, father, sister and brother when I truly needed you the most.

Thank you for all the hard times that I had to endure, because you had a purpose and a plan for all of it. I will continue to keep my hand in your hand, and stay close to you.

You have never left me, nor forsaken me, and you have always been there to carry me and see me thorough. Family and friends may have walked away, but you, Lord, have been there every step of the way.

I love you, Lord, and I will continue to lift my voice, cry out to you, and give you all of me so that I may be used and be a blessing to all. Now use me, Lord, as your servant, and draw me nearer every day, because I am willing to run for you, Jesus, all the way. If I should fall down while I am doing your will, Lord, don't be angry with me, just pick me up, dust me off, and send me on the path that you have for me. I am willing, dear Jesus, to run all the way for you till the very end.

Thank you to the man that God brought in my life and stood by my side, Joe. The one man here on earth who loves me in spite of all my flaws. You found me when I was lost and all alone. I prayed for a great man, and God heard my prayer. You have been my friend for so many years, but all I did was stand in fear. You have provided for me and brought me out of the rain, and I am not ashamed to say that I love you and thank you from the bottom of my heart.

Thank you to my children Roderick, Quintin, Xzavia, Sandy and Demarcus for being my inspiration, keeping me afloat, and never giving up on me even through my tears and all of my many fears. Even through my hardest times, my surgeries and all my many ups and downs, you all have truly been there for me, and I love you.

Thank you to Pastor Maverick Gayden, Kathy Gayden, Lashonda (shorty), Aunt Jackie Bowen, Darleen, Panola and Linda. And not to forget the two ladies at JPS Hospital in Fort Worth Enid Malbrough and Veronica Brown, Wow to you two women for standing by my side and allowing me to cry on your shoulders, and being there in all my struggles. When I needed you all the most, you never turned a deaf ear to me, and you stood by my side through my difficult times.

Thank you to my close friends Ronnie and Rosalind Jones who stuck by me when everyone else gave up on me. Through all the long nights when I cried and felt like I wanted to give up, you encouraged me to press on, and let me know that the Lord still fights my battles all the way.

Thank you to the many people who have supported me the many times I came to you with my head held down. God, I love you and you will always be the head of my life, and always in my heart. I am no longer a scorned woman; I am a woman of God. Amen.

Dedication

In loving memory of my mother, Betty Jean (Jackson) McCray. To my grandsons, Elisha Huckaby and Zamarion Henderson; my husband Joe Louis Blackshear; my children Roderick Lynn Huckaby Jr., Quintin Von and Sandy Huckaby, Demarcus and Xzavia Ward-Johnson. To my grandchildren Isaiah, Zachariah (Zac), Gabriella, Keilen, Kamaren and Arryiah (Tink).

To God, who allowed me to have the gift of wisdom, patience, productive womanhood, consistency, kindness, and love.

Contents

Acknowledgments 3
Words from the Heart 9
"Feelings of what I felt" 15
My Secret 17
Woman 27
Thoughts of a Woman 31
Shattered dreams 35
Troubled Times 37
The Big Move 47
The Night that Changed Everything 55
The Night I Will Never Forget 59
Women Don't Give Up 65
I'm Gonna Hold On 67
I am grateful 69
I Am Healed 73
This Place 75
Worthy to be Praised 79
I Want You to Know 81
No Separation of Love 85
So They Say 87
Touch of Real Love 89
Trust 91
 I'll Make It 93
Hold on, Child 97
Sorry 101

Love	103
Brighter Day	105
To be Kept by Jesus	107
Nobody but God	109
What Kinda Journey	113
Still Here	117
Scorned Woman	119
It's All About You	133
A Lost Son	145
When the Control of a Man Began	151
Man is This?	155
A Man of Explosion	157
Materialistic Man of God	161
Speak to Me	163
When God Chose Me	165
When the Storms are Raging in My Life	169
The Move that Broke the Chains	171
Learning to live again	177
If Only You Could Know	185
Imagine	187
No More Tears on My Pillow	189
God Can	191
G C W W S I P	195
The Strength, Struggle and Power that God Gives	197
Through the Eyes of a Woman Who Made it Through	201
Living for a purpose	203
The Untold Secret	205
When Daddy Calls	211
Revelation 3:8	215
The Day that I Met My Natural Father	217
A Love I Once Had	221
So Glad I Made It	223
Shoes	225
End of a Chapter	227

Words from the Heart

To the women of this nation, may my book, which is filled with words from the heart, my thoughts, verses and small poems, be an inspiration to you all. May this book be an inspiration to many who may be struggling and can't see their way through.

To my heavenly father who sits high and looks low, God you are the author of this book and I thank you for my life, health, and strength just being who you are to me and my family and friends. God, I love you and honor you, and I want to give you all the praises to you and you alone. This I ask in Jesus's name is that you Lord, help me to write down the true words on paper so that I can show your women that although the storms of life come and sometimes strong and hard it is you who will if they seek you carry them all the way through.

I will give you all the honor and the glory because it belongs to you, and I will go ahead and give you all the praise in advance for what you have done in my life, and where you have brought me from and Yes where you will lead me and see me through. This I ask in Jesus's name to the Almighty one who is the creator of All heaven and earth, God I thank you. Amen

Amen and Amen

And Jabez called on the God of Israel, saying, Oh that thou wouldest bless me indeed, and enlarge my coast, and that thine hand might be with me, and that thou wouldest keep me from evil, that it may not grieve me! And God granted him that which he that it may not grieve me! And God granted him that which he requested.

1 Chronicles 4:10, King James Version (KJV)

On October 4, 1967, a young woman from a small country town in East Texas gave birth to a beautiful baby girl. She wed a young Army gentleman who was somewhat older than her. They were in love, regardless of the age difference. She was still in high school, but preparing to graduate. The young woman and gentleman were my mother and father. My father wed my mother, and took her from the small country town and brought her to the city of Fort Worth, Texas. I don't know much about what my mother and father went through or even what their childhood life was like, because they never talked about it with me; the little that I do know came from my aunts and cousins. My mother never really paid much attention to me as a child, and she never hugged or kissed me much. I had a sister who was two years younger than me, and a baby brother who died at birth. I remember my mom being sad and crying a lot, and my dad seemed to believe she made herself that way.

As I grew up, there were a lot of differences in the house between my sister and me. I never understood why, and I would always ask, "How come you pay more attention to my sister than you do me? Momma, why is it that my sister always gets things that she wants?" But I never got a good answer from her.

Now don't get me wrong, she gave us a lot of toys around the holidays and blessed us with good clothes and shoes for our feet, and the essentials along with food and a wonderful house. My parents took very good care of us in making sure we had what we needed to live, and sent us to private school before we ended up in public schooling. I do recall that sometimes I would have to take the wrath of the things my sister did yes it would hurt, and I felt like I was always by myself. Most of the time, my mom would take my sister with her and I was left with my father. My daddy would call me stupid and say things to me like, "You will be just like your mom, and you will never amount to anything. You are just dumb." I heard those words so much that they started to penetrate my mind, and I would say to myself, You know, I just might not be anything. It was really around middle school when I began to feel a great deal of what my daddy said to me.

When my father would punish me, he would thump me on my forehead repeatedly or whip me. Whenever he whipped me, it would leave big welts on my body and sometimes blood would seep out. They hurt so bad I would just scream. He would take the switches, belt, or even a whip that he got when we went on a trip to Mexico, and whip me, cursing at the same time until he was tired. I'd tell him it hurt, but he would never stop, and my momma never came to my rescue. I didn't know why. I never really remember him whipping my sister at all, but this one time he tried to whip the both of us because we were too loud for him. He told us to be quiet, but we just wanted to play in our rooms and have sister fun. We got away from him, and he did not like that.

I grew up and started seeking out what my friends were doing, and I thought that they were having so much fun. I tried to find friends that would take me for who I was or try to fit in. I would do things that I knew were not right, but I just wanted to be liked. I wanted to be loved, to feel wanted and feel good about myself, but that was not always the case. We could not talk on the phone hardly or go to friends' houses or away from our parents unless it was over to a relative's house. I would try to talk to as many friends as I could while I was at school, because

I knew when I arrived home, that would be the end of having all outside communication.

My dad was verbally and physically abusive to my mom as well. It hardly ever felt like we had a happy home, and when he was mad I did not feel safe. There was so much screaming and fighting in the house. One day I recall my parents getting into an altercation and my dad did the most horrible things to my mom. He beat and choked her with his bare fist. After that, I never thought of my dad as being a great man again. I believed no man should ever do what he did to my mom, and he should have paid for that.

"Feelings of what I felt"

When God blesses a man with a woman, she is to be cherished as a queen, and she is to stand right beside that man and treat him like her king. She is to be his friend and should be able to confide in him, as well as he confides in her. Respect should be given and reciprocated, and no one should be given access into the circle that was only meant for husband, wife, and God. A husband, or wife (Because women are abusive, too!), is not to put their hands on the other to slap or kick, or let their fist go upside the other's head, face, or body just to get the attention that you demand from them. This is not what anyone should do to someone whom they say they love. That is exactly the type of household that I resided in and to me, that is abuse no matter how you look at it.

I love my mom. She was an independent woman who worked and completed some schooling. She worked for a great assembly plant in Arlington, Texas, and enjoyed bringing home her own money and not having to solely depend on my dad. I look back and realize that when she went to work, that was her happy time. But then she had to come home. When there was an argument and my father hit my mom and did other things to her, my sister and I tried to intervene to help her, but my dad would just try to hit us. I would say to myself, I wish he would go somewhere, and I hope his hands fall off and he is never able to use them again. I wanted him to go away and never come back. Then maybe my mom would be happy, and this home we lived in would be happy, with big smiles, love, and lots of laughter.

It seemed my thoughts and dreams of wishing my daddy away were about to come true. As I recall, I was attending McLean Middle School in Fort Worth, Texas in 1978-1979. My mom and dad were separating. As they were going through the very bad divorce, my dad would say tormenting and hurtful things about our mom. On one occasion, he came to pick us up and as we were exiting the driveway, he told us that we would never see our mom again. As he said this, we were in middle of the street and cars were coming, but my sister and I exited the car while it was moving and ran back to the house screaming. "Momma, help us!" we shouted as we banged on the door and set off the house alarm. "Help us! He is trying to take us away, and he won't bring us back." Mom came to the door with her gun and told my dad some choice words, and he went away. My mom and dad finalized their divorce, and things were never the same with our broken up family again.

My Secret

I entered middle school and thought that this would be a new beginning because I was now in public school, and that meant maybe I could meet some real friends who would like me just for me. I wanted to fit in, and I thought that if I could just be myself, they would like me. I thought wrong, because the people that I went to school with were not from the side that I was from. Just because I wore nice clothes and talked funny, they said I did not fit in with them. Oh how I wished I had a good friend to sit, talk, and laugh with.

There was another woman that was close in my life my mother's sister who I was around often because she did not work and when our parents needed her she was around to assist. I did love my aunt a lot because I admire the lovely things she did with her daughter as she took time out with her showing love and showing her how much her daughter meant to her. My cousin was around the same age as I was but one thing about her my aunt felt that she never did wrong and she was considered the little perfect angel that everyone loves. I felt as I was around my aunt and cousin it was always a competition and I was the one who was always at the bottom because in my aunts eyes her daughter did nothing she saw wrong, a perfect angel, but that angel will later as I grew older saw what my aunt thought would one day be something great, marry somebody great would hurt her mother's heart, and I would be the one if I was around take places she needed to go and still give the love and respect from a niece to her aunt. I also had to prove myself around my aunt, and that was not easy, even though she said she loved me, she would say bad things about me and I received enough of that from home.

There was this boy who lived not too far from me in the neighborhood. He didn't go to school with me, but I'd see him all the time while going back and forth to school. I didn't really know him, but I thought he was a good gentleman. Sometimes he'd be over to the lady's house that used to watch us. One day, he asked me to come over to his house and visit him. I was about fourteen years old at the time. I went over without anyone knowing where I was and thought it was okay, because he said his mom would be home; plus, he was known and respected around the family and neighborhood. When I walked inside, he told me his mom was in her room at the back of the house. We sat down and began to talk. I felt comfortable because that was exactly what I was looking for, a friend that I could talk to and laugh with.

As we sat on the couch talking and laughing, he came close to me and began to force himself on me. I told him several times to stop or I would yell out to his mom, but he just told me to shut up. "You will not tell anyone what we did," he said. I remember having to fight him for what felt like was an eternity, begging him to stop. He grabbed my arm and twisted it to my back. He was going under my clothes, and I screamed, "Stop, you are hurting me! Help!" I screamed so that his mom could hear, not knowing she wasn't even in the house. He threw me down on the floor, and I hit the ground really hard. I was screaming, "Anyone, please!" But no one was there, even though I could hear the TV in the back. Then he forced himself in me, and I said, "Stop, it hurts." He was holding me down and sayings "Shut up and take it. No one will ever believe you if you tell so just take it and shut up, girl."

Once it was over, I ran home and went straight to the

bathroom to get in some water, because I was bleeding, and hurting badly. I hopped in the tub and sat in the water, crying and telling myself that no one could ever know because I would not be able to tell anyone, not even my mom. I knew she wouldn't believe me and she would only say, "You knew better than going over there, so what did you expect?" I did not tell anyone my secret, even though it hurt me and I needed to tell what that boy did to me. It bothered me so much that I could not sleep.

As the days went on, I felt different inside and I did not trust anyone. I wanted to be loved, but not like that.

I attended South West High School in Fort Worth, Texas, and once again I wanted to fit in with the popular crowd. I did not want to be an outcast and be lonely. Everybody was going to a friend's house during lunch hour at school. I went along, and we were having a great time. There were no parents around, and there was a guy there that I really wanted to talk to. I remember seeing him at school, and he would smile at me every time we crossed paths. My heart would jump and I would get so excited. I thought that he was very cute and nice, so I was amazed to know that he liked me too.

Everyone was playing games and watching TV, but I was ready to go back to school before the next class started. I asked around to see if anyone was going back. The guy heard me and said, " I'm going back. I can let you ride with me." We were on our way back to school when he veered off the path. I said, "Hey, where are we going? You turned off, and the school is not this way."

He said, "We are going, don't worry about it." I remember him pulling over, and he said, "We are just going to stop for a second. I just want to ask you something." I got a sick feeling in the pit of my stomach. He said, "I like you and I do know you like me, so how about us getting to know each other?" His knowing each other was not what I had in mind, because he began to touch me, and I said, "No, I want to go to school."

He said, "I will take you to school after you give me what I want." I said, "No, and I do mean no. I don't want to do that. I do like you, but we have to get to know one another."

He said, "This is how I get to know the girls I like."

"Well, I don't do this, and I want you to take me to school," I said. But that was not what he wanted, so he jumped over and was trying to take my clothes off. He hit me and hurt me really badly, and forced himself on me. When it was over and I was back at school, I did not go to the classroom. Instead, I went in the bathroom and hid in a stall. I was hurting physically, but more so mentally, and I didn't know what to do or even who to tell. *Hide it, Tonya, just hide it and don't tell. They will just say you deserved it because you should not have even left with him or even left the school. What do I do? Why does this keep happening to me? Did I do something bad? Maybe I should just do it, and I would not have to suffer as much,* I thought. I did not say anything and again decided to keep this to myself, and not tell anyone. I just kept thinking, *what is wrong with you? You have serious problems and need help. Why do you let yourself get hurt? Are you really stupid like your dad said?*

So I pushed that and all of the bad situations that were occurring in my life to the back of my mind, and I pressed my way on and tried to enjoy school. As I was focusing on school and enjoying playing in the Southwest concert band, I started talking to a young man that lived in my neighborhood who had previously wanted to be of acquaintance with me. He was a great gentleman, and he did not force himself on me nor try to do things to me that I did not want. He was raised in a respectable two-parent home, and to me it seemed like it was a loving home whenever I would go to visit. We ended up being very close, and he did things that a gentleman would do for a young lady he wanted to date. Every time we went places he would open my door first to make sure I was in safe and secure. Walk me to my class every period as we both attend the same school, because there was guys that I did not like and would always mess with me as I walk to and from my classes, and this gave me relief knowing that there was someone there who showed they cared for my safety. Buying me things that a young girl does not have to ask for and showing me a good time to the special events that were taken place in the school, was something that would make a young girl of my age happy, and feeling safe and secure with him meant a lot in my book. Yes that is a true gentleman.

I ended up getting pregnant at the age of 16. He was a planned baby by the both of us because we did on several occasions speak about what we can do to stay together and make us happy. Was this a good decision some would say straight forward No because you both are still young kids in school who need to be planning ahead for a great future, and that is not with having a baby to raise early with no source of means to take care the baby and of all the needs that will occur when you have a baby. Even though it was wrong, this is what I wanted to make me feel like I had somebody to love and take care of. I knew it would be hard and I had no job to support him, but I was thinking I just wanted to love and be loved. We really did not know when we were going to plan the baby and if we would stick to the plan we just knew we talked and when the time arrives it will just happen and we will not have any regrets. The one thing that stayed with us was that no one can break the bond we were building together so that I will never feel the hurt from anyone else and we can bring a little bundle of joy in our lives at the same time to love also.

So as I continued to date the young man my love grew stronger and I felt he was the only one that would hear me and be there for me when I was having trouble at home, and that was at the time as a young teenager I felt a gentlemen to me, but not knowing as I grew older what a real gentlemen really is, and how you are to be treated by one. The knowledge is growing up and getting older and going through the rough times in your life you will know what the definition of gentlemen really means.

So at the tender age of fifteen years of age when I conceived, but I was sixteen when I had my first son, I remember my mom, when she found out, and how mad she was. She even told me at one point that she wished I was never born and she hated me. "I wish you weren't ever here; you are a disgrace," she said.

I wondered if that was what her mom said to her when she got pregnant. I would say to my mom, "Why do you treat me like this? Do you really love me?" She would say, "Girl, go on. Get out of my face, and go and sit down." Months went by, and we both were excited about the baby and I would be very excited and happy if I had a girl but as you know all men want their first born to be a boy. I still attended regular high school, but the counselor wanted me to attend a school for pregnant girls so that I would not get hurt and still be able to go to the doctors' appointments and finish on time. I refused to go to the New Lives School for pregnant girls located in Fort Worth and remained at the current school attending classes and passing grades. My main focus was on the baby and telling myself I will never treat my baby as my parents did me, I will love him unconditionally and show that love and not just with words. As I was growing and getting bigger my mom was still distant and my boyfriend would take me to my obstetrician appointment after the first initial one my mom took me to first after receiving the doctor information from my boyfriend's mom who recently had a baby, and that doctor came highly recommended. My dad was upset when he found out but later took it all in and took me to buy clothes that would fit me so I would have appropriate attire for school, and I then said umm my dad really loves me in his own way, but sometimes his ways are hurtful to me physically and mentally. In the second semester of school in my twelfth grade year, I had to attend school a half a day due to having over the amount of credits needed to graduate, so at twelve o'clock my boyfriend and I would take lunch and then go home where I was alone. But I was fine with that because what we planned together was about to come true real soon. We were about to have a beautiful baby to love, and I still was being selfish because I knew that I really could not take care of the baby. My main concern was that I get to love someone who will love me back no matter how I am. I graduated early, but had to wait for the initial graduation day which my boyfriend and I both attended in 1985. I had the baby right before I graduated thinking that I would still be pregnant and would have to walk across the stage looking like I was a big whale out of the ocean. The precious baby arrived and we could not have been happier, even my mom who said the crazy things she said but when she saw her first grandson it changed her just a little but more love for the baby not me, all still stayed the same and sometime got worse

I told myself that if I got married I could leave home, and I would have someone to love me. So we both sat down and decided to get married as he went out and received a job to take care of us I was still at home with mom planning our wedding with no money. I could not take the constant put down and the mistreatment of what I was enduring at home and feeling bad about myself so I too went and received a job that would help the three of us to move and take care of our needs. Yes it all came together when we told our family we were getting married so his family and mine came together to put what we thought would be a small wedding together turned out to be a big one that every girl dreamed of. My sister was in my wedding and my best friend as well as his friends of his choice and it was beautiful with family and friends, and yes my baby was there to take our first family portraits. Once we were married, we moved into our own apartment in Everman Texas and it was a townhouse that was fully furnished by both sides of the family. Soon and very soon the once love of my life the man that I cherished the most my perfect gentlemen would turn into someone I did not see, a mad man hiding beneath, pretending to be the great man would show me early into the marriage how a bad situation can rise quickly within a blink of an eye. My husband did not want to work, and I found out that he was doing drugs. I told him that was not the life style that I wanted to raise my baby in, but little did I know, I was pregnant again, even though I was on the pill, and this means that my children when this baby is born will be eleven-a- half months apart. I ended up having to call my mom and this would be the first time I involved her in my problems because I knew that she would not care. I came home from a hard day of working at Carls Jr Resturant and I was not feeling my best and wanted to pick up the baby from the daycare he attended go home and rest. To my surprise, that would not happen. No Tonya no rest for you, only confusion waiting, lurking about to cause you heartaches, tears and fears of what lies ahead for you a baby and the unborn baby you were carrying. Went to the townhome and tried to turn the lock to unlock the door and before I could unlock the door my husband the father of my baby opened the door with a slight crack in it and told me to go away and come back later. He would not let me in the house because he had people in there doing drugs, and I knew he was doing something that was not right because I smelled a fowl odor reeking of an unpleasant smoke but not the smoke of a cigarette. My husband as I heard women voices as the laughter fill the atmosphere told me go come back and he at that time slammed the door in my face and I was unable to get into my own home. Now the only thing I could think of was to go get my mother and tell her what was taking place and what do I need to do. My mom followed me back to the house along with her best friend her peace that will pass all understanding her 45 weapon told me to stay in the car and she will go and handle this matter. I did not want my mom in trouble nor did I want anything to happen to her, so I traveled right behind her and watched her as she banged on the door with the barrel of the weapon. My husband answered but did not want to open the door, as he told my mom that was his house and go away. My mom took me home, and with just the little items we had and told me I can do better and plus now you are pregnant again and you do not need that drama in your life so you will need to separate from him and do better with your life, and you can only stay here for a short time and yes that time was short because my mom would always argue with me and I then said no I will not put up with this. So I filed for a divorce and could not receive until after my second baby was born, so I just went to work and did what I knew best while in my mom's house and that was to stay to myself until the time comes for me to vacate with my children and that needed to be real soon. I knew that I had to move out of my mom's house quickly because she would not treat me right, and it would be hard for the both of us and my babies, so I found an apartment and moved to the Woodhaven area and at that time it was a great area and safe area to live as I was a single woman with two small children. Thinking back, had I really focused on what the true meaning of living for the future and preparing so I will not have to struggle, maybe even going through the rough times, I would have sucked it up and made the best out of a bad situation so that I could have what I really needed to take care of my needs as well as my wants. Only being married to my husband for not even a little of one month and a half was the worst mistake of my life, but I did receive the most wonderful and precious gifts from God above, my boys. It hurt me a lot to relinquish someone that I really thought would be with me forever, but he put a brick through my heart and left me to raise two boys on my own. Hurt was something that had followed me for a while, and I wanted it to just go away.

(Saying)

No More Shackles

No More Am I Bound

No More Being Held Down

See, I Am Free

The Chains Are Gone From Me

Woman

Inspiration to all women

As a woman, I try hard each and every day to fulfill what my expectations are. As a woman, I am a girl, daughter, young lady, mother, and wife, and yes, a woman. This woman sometimes feels that her cup is overfilled and there is no ending to it. I make myself daily move forward knowing that if I don't, my job will never be done. I know that it is the Lord who gives me the strength to keep going forth on my daily journey. Regardless of what color you are, you are still a woman, and you try your best to fit in wherever you can. Sometimes in the middle of your tribulations, you find yourself in places, and you don't even know how you got there, but you overcame those obstacles with a smile on your face, knowing that you still have the strength to pursue all that is placed in front of you. Not giving up the fight is what you strive for. Determination is the key to it all, and you will go through whatever means necessary to make it work. Whatever is poured in your lap you take and don't say a complaining word. Instead, you complete the job that was set before you.

To the women who feel like they could not go on, there is a man who sits high ad looks low, and he will see you through if you just give it all to him and leave it alone. The battles and the bruises that we go through are just a test for us, and after a while we will be able to tell another woman who is going through hard times that she can and will make it through. Stand tall and strong and know that the master is on your side; even in the hour of your weakness, he will bring you through. Ask God to hold you and not let go. As tired as we may get—weary and filled with hurt—we get up, dust ourselves off, and walk into the womanhood of life that God intended for us, meaning the role that all women take when they reach maturity.

Is there any hope for us? Any relief in sight? Can we accept what comes our way? Can we tell ourselves that we can make it and hold our head up to the victory that lies waiting for us? Can and will we be able to rejoice at the end of the storm knowing that until we get there, the water will roar and the mountains will get high, and the valleys will get wide, but we women can be strong enough to endure it all?

I say to all you women of the nation: hold on and don't give up on yourself. Fight for what you believe in and fight for what is right. Don't give up on life and don't let go of what you know is right. Call on the one true man who is and will be there for you and help you to stand strong and tall. Women, we were made to be strong and take what comes our way, and yes we can, but there is that side that we have, where we have to step aside and let the man of God take over and be the head. Walk into what he has for you when you do walk with the dignity and the pride that you have as a woman and be strong. Teach women from city to city, and nation to nation, regardless of their race, how to lean on one another and know that if we all come together, we can learn what to do when the bad times hit us hard. Yes, women, we will struggle and go through trying times, but if we lean and depend on one another and help one another and, most of all lean on God, we will be strong and make it through. We are fighters, and we will win when we have the captain on our side. Trust and believe he will see us through, and in the end we will say that we are more than conquerors. Women, stay strong, be bold, hold on. A change is coming, and the Lord will see you through.

PSALM 20 (KJV)
The Lord hears thee in the day of trouble; the
name of the God of Jacob defends thee;
Send thee help from the sanctuary, and
strengthen thee out of Zion;
Remember all thy offerings, and accept
thy burnt sacrifice; Selah.
We will rejoice in thy salvation, and in the name of our God
we will set up our banners: the LORD fulfills all thy petitions.
Now know I that the LORD saveth his anointed;
he will hear him from his holy heaven with
the saving strength of his right hand.
Some trust in chariots, and some in horses: but we
will remember the name of the LORD our God.
They are brought down and fallen: but
we are raised and stand upright
Save, LORD: let the king hear us when we call.

Thoughts of a Woman

There are some things in my life that I had to go through and did not understand why this was allowed. Lord, please help me to overcome and help me with my fears and go through my trials, dear God. Your will is what I have to go through, and now I understand why the toils and trials of this life have taken me to another level that I never knew existed. I have been through many trials and dangers in my life, and by the grace of God I have made it through. His grace and mercy will, and have followed me throughout this long journey in my life.

Yet I am still young and have many more hills to climb, but with God on my side I will not fail. Though the scars have been healed by cream and bandages, God's love I still will remember. Yet I will not forget that it reminds me that I have Jesus who has brought me through the rugged terrains once was scorned and broken but now I am healed.

The winds blew and the storms came hard. I watched the leaves blow off the branches and a small tornado rip the house, shredding it to tiny pieces. I saw myself sometimes going down just like that tree when the storm hit. But oh how I made it by God's mercy and his wonderful grace.

Life throws a stumbling block in your way, but you have to stand tall, strong, and firm to what is and how it will and watch the change occur. If you give it all to God and know that He will never leave you nor forsake you, He will be there till the bitter sweet end.

I am a woman who has been hurt, battered, beaten, and bruised sometimes to the point where I just wanted to give up, but I made it. Yes, Tonya Michelle made it through the storms that were raging in my life both day and night. I had to say, God, I know you see what I'm going through. When will it all end? When will my life begin?

I heard Him call my name one day, and I had to answer. I was glad that I did because now I feel so free. Free from the pain, the guilt, the sorrow, free from being hurt, free from the beating, and free from being scorned.

To all you ladies, who feel as though you are feeling the abuse, the neglect, and ridicule, hold your head up and know that God is on your side, standing next to you to carry you all the way. He will never leave you nor forsake you, so give it to him and put your head on the pillow and go to sleep knowing that God has it all under control.

Let go and let God fix it, and after a while you won't have to struggle, cry, feel lonely, depressed, sad, or even miserable because He will bring sunshine to your life, and rainbows will follow thereafter.

As I once heard two ladies say, "To all you sons of motherless goats, to all you dark chocolate Christmas cookie eating fools," to mess with one of God's women is like putting your head in a furnace and turning up the heat, so leave me alone before I put you in the hands of all hands that will truly take care of you who would be God. Meaning if you play or mess with a woman of God you are bound to have her place you in the hands of the almighty so He will have the last say over what you have done to her. So, women, I say don't give up and don't fear, because trouble lasts but yet a small season, because joy will come in the morning and the pain will leave. The scars remain, but as long as you have Jesus you don't have to worry about anything, Nor will you fall. Give it all to the Lord and stand still, tall, and firm and watch what he can do for you.

Shattered dreams

Shattered dreams. My dreams then, but not my dreams now. The dreams that I once believed that were to come true felt like the dreams that truly passed me by within a blink of an eye. My dreams that I held so dear, thinking that all I had to do was believe and wish all would come true for me. Oh how I lost all those dreams and feelings. Like all they did were pass me by; my shattered dreams. Dreams that felt like someone came and stole them away in the middle of the night while I lay fast asleep. Even when my doors were locked from the inside, how, oh how, did they get in? Who let them in to steal what I thought was once mine, but never to see again? My shattered dreams.

I used to think that when you have a man you have everything. You give your whole life, world, and even your soul, trusting and believing that you have something great, not knowing in the end that person will shatter all that you believed and trusted in to be happy for eternity. I trusted you, I gave you my all and you truly betrayed me and you let me down. I thought that we were going to be together forever, but you stole my heart and tried to steal my mind, and used me like a dirty wash cloth and threw me in a corner to be hidden from the world. Hide me, you did, and only brought me out when it was convenient for you, for your pleasure and enjoyment. Hid me and took me off the shelf to take me places where it made you look good in the eyes of others, but only made me feel like less of a woman. God did not make me to be this person. He made me to be greater than I ever thought.

No more shattered dreams, no more loneliness or hurt will I let you store upon me and tear me down to where I feel not even the man upstairs can help. I have risen and looked to the hills and fell down on my knees and asked the almighty to help me, fix me and fill me once again with the love, joy, comfort and peace in my heart and in my mind. Help me to know that the dreams that I store in my heart and lay on the table before you can be the dreams that will truly come to life. If I give my father up in Heaven my heart, soul and mind and believe in Him, He will surely take care of me.

No more shattered dreams will I have to face. The Lord states that if we just trust and believe in Him, He will take all our fears and tears away and place a wonderful smile on our face. Knowing that the Lord is my light, I will never have to fear anything.

So now I have given the Lord all of me, and I asked him to hide me from all things that try to take me away from my dreams and the things that he has in store for me. What is for me will be for me; I do know that now. Not to put my trust in man, but only in the Lord.

Yes, I walk with my head high and I have no doubt in my mind that the Lord brought me from the dark valley into the light of a new day. So I smile and trust and believe in all that I set myself out to do, giving it to the Lord, stepping back and watching the miracle of the master do his work before my eyes. No more shattered dreams do I have. No more shattered dreams do I live for. I will stay positive and focus on what the Lord has for me to do, and I will do just that, His will and not mine. No more shattered dreams for me.

Troubled Times

When I was seventeen years of age and some months I remember moving out but going to stay with my dad's sister because I had nowhere to go was a big help in my life. My aunt was a great woman who at any time I needed her she was always there and I love her for that. She never judged me or talked about me and I admired her because she was a single woman who raised and took care of her children all by herself and I saw that and knew that I can do the same for my babies too. My aunt knew that I had nowhere to go and I was just about to have my baby and that was already hard for me, but somehow I was strong and knew I would make it just did not know how but knew in my heart I was about to have two children and I will take care of them and love them unconditionally. I knew that once my baby was born I will be able to seek a place for my family and start a new life and knew that it was not going to be easy but I knew I had to grow up really quick and prove to myself that I can do it and I will be the best mother to my children and love them unlike my mother did to me given little or no love. I finally after the baby was born in 1986 was able to get a little job but it did not pay enough so yes I struggled daily, but to have my own place with nothing barely in the refrigerator and sleeping on the floor but to have just a little peace in my life and not have anything was better than being humiliated, torn down and ridiculed all the time.

On my own leaving the nest getting my own place and raising

my two boys, I was the ultimate struggle but I had to make the job I had work for me until something better came along I managed to make it through. Being young and raising two boys had its challenges saying to myself everyday as they grow will I be able to endure raising boys with no man in my life? My father who raised me would come around and help me with the needs of the boys and I; and every time he pop up at my house he would always say things to me that I hated to hear. He would always yell, scream, and curse at me and call me names that a father should never call his daughter. He told me I was not and would never be anything, and call me a whore. It made it hard for me to even try to ask or even talk to him whenever I needed something. Although he did help me sometimes, I would have to endure the terrible lectures and name calling in order to receive what I needed for me and my children. My mother's help was limited, which was okay. What I wanted more was her love and a mother-daughter relationship with her. She did help me with my boys though, by providing some of the essential needs for them, as far as clothes, Christmas and birthday gifts, which was much appreciated. I loved her regardless of the relationship that had come about. Now don't get me wrong, I loved my parents a great deal, but the things that were said and done to me put me in a bad space that stayed with me for a while.

As the years went on, I kept trying to find a man but always found the wrong one. I just did not want to be by myself. I was trying to fill a void in my life that I know now was the lack of love that I did not receive from my parents, which took me down a devastating path. So I started being promiscuous, going from man to man. This behavior went on for two years when I ran across a man who I really liked and that was the beginning year of 1988. The only problem is that he was married. Still, I ended up getting pregnant and I told him, "I don't want to hurt your wife, so I will do what is best and go. I don't want to do anything to cause more hurt than I already have to your family." I had deep feelings for him, but he was not mine, and I could never cause so much pain. So I decided to raise our baby by myself so he could go with his family. He was not pleased with this and agreed with me saying that he has rights to the baby when the baby is born, and he will not leave me alone. During my pregnancy I endured hard time with this man because he would show up at my house to let me know he will not leave and he wanted to be with me, but once I said again I said I did not need you I will leave you alone and I will not ask for any money or help from you. I knew that I got into something that I should not have crossed into so I decided to change the situation and make it easy for him and hopefully his wife will not find out about the baby, but she did and she was not happy and that caused great confusion and heartaches. The wife said to me I knew he was married with a family, and yes I did but at that time I was only thinking about my needs and no one else.

I had my baby girl and two wonderful boys, and that was my life. My mom watched my boys when I went to the hospital but my best friend had to pick them up from her because they could not stay there with her until I leave the hospital with the baby. I also had a really good friend that was like a big brother to me who helped me with my boys during my hospital stay and that meant the world to me having to not worry about who will help me with the boys while I am here having the baby. He was there for me when I had no one else to depend on. I was used to not having my family around, and it did not bother me. I would tell myself, "Tonya, it is okay." It was hurtful and many times I cried, but through it all the ones that were by my side were there for me all the way.

I tried even after the baby came to go ahead and involve the man I got involved with and his wife in the baby's life and the wife accepted the baby, but in doing so by dropping the baby off I just felt this would not be in the best interest of the baby nor the wife and that made me feel uneasy. Listening to family and friends saying I would not take my baby over to their house you don't really know how the wife feels. I took all what I was told held onto it and said to myself I will not cause any more trauma so I will call him and tell him its ok he does not buy the baby anything and has never bought her anything all she had was what I bought with just the little money I had. The wife did buy something for the baby but I felt that it was not her responsibility and he wanted the baby in his life but did nothing that would not fly with me, so I said no more will you lay eyes on her.

One day when I was at home, my baby's daddy came by. He kicked my door in with rage and fight in him and stormed to my bedroom. I called the police, and he was hauled off to jail. During this time I would say to myself, *I can do all things through Christ who gives me the strength.* I cried out to the Lord to help me because this was too hard for me, but I would not give up, nor would I give in, because I put myself in this mess and only the Lord could help me. So I went and applied for public assistance because I wasn't working, and I was living in my dad's rent house. I was very appreciative of that, but there was a great big "but" in that one also. See, my dad was a very controlling person, and if he helps you then you will have to do as he says.

Finally, I applied for a particular job and was hired on. Although it was a part-time job, it helped me a great deal with my children. I received the job with the FWISD as a bus driver and the only downside was that in the summer there was no work, so you either found a second income, or, if you were lucky, you may have a summer route to help you make it, or you would have to file for assistance. While employed there, I met a friend. She was a sweet young lady, but little did I know she was out there in the world. Regardless of everything she was into, she was a great friend and was like a dear sister that I never had. Her mom was closer to me than my own mom. My friend and her mom liked me for who I was, not for what they wanted me to be. I worked at the bus company, and I was so excited. I was in my early twenties, and my children were little babies. It was hard for me to provide for my children. Daycare alone was a great bill and

I was barely making enough money to cover that.

As the years went by, I met a young man who I wish to this day never had entered in my life. I met this gentleman who I thought was my king. He was so nice, so sweet to me. He even adored my children. I was thinking, *Oh yes he is the one and this will be a long, lasting relationship. He is kind, sweet, and a great gentleman.* Although I can honestly say I had some doubts about him, I pushed them back and went on with the relationship. I didn't really talk to him and avoided him for a while, because I had some trust issues. While I was dating this gentleman, one of my friends was killed in a car accident, and it was devastating. It was like losing a close family member.

I would go over to her house, she and her children and her family would welcome my babies and I with open arms. Now, my friend was married, but her husband was not around as much whenever I would visit. I did see him a time or two when she would have gatherings and he seemed to be a nice man. She never talked a lot about him to us.

When my friend died, I did not know her husband would try something that should have never entered his mind. We left the cemetery, after putting my best friend to rest, I rode along with her children in the family car back to the house. I was asked to stay around and help out with the children to make sure they were okay, because they'd just buried their mom and they were young. I did just that and stayed around to assist with the children, along with mine. Once the children were settled I decided to take a nap because I was tired.

I went to lay down on the couch in the den in the back of the house while the kids were down for a nap. As I began to drift off, my friend's husband came and sat next to me. I asked him if there was anything wrong and if I needed to do something, knowing that he was grieving because of the loss of his wife. Before I could ask anything else, he stated, "Yes, I want you to help me with something." I asked what, but he did not say a word. Then he started mumbling like he was trying to say something and crying. All of a sudden, he grabbed me and tried to kiss me. I slapped him and pushed him off, and I screamed. I told him, "How can you do this when your wife was my best friend and we just buried her?"

He said with no shame, "She is gone. It is okay. You can help me out."

I gathered my things and my babies, promising never to return. I asked myself why and how do I even get in those situations, and I know in that moment I did nothing wrong. I looked and evaluated myself. Did I say something? Did I do something to make him think he could go there with me? I don't recall doing anything. I never said anything and kept what happened to myself. I felt that if I told someone, they would blame me. They would say I led him on, and try to judge something that was not true. Or they would say that I put myself in that predicament so I got what I deserved. I heard that all the time.

I decided to go back to the man I met and put all my focus on him. Unfortunately, I could not see what I needed to, only what I wanted to. That caused so much pain in the end. I ended up losing my apartment because I was not making enough with daycare and other essentials, so the young man and I decided to move in together. Now I understand that you must be married to be blessed and not shack, because God frowns on that. We ended up moving from place to place, wherever and whatever we could afford. We moved in with his mom, which was an experience in itself. I remember one day they had a family gathering, and that family loved to drink and smoke. I knew this man cared about me. He said he loved me, and he always hugged me and talked to me, until one day everything changed within the blink of an eye. At the family gathering, my babies were outside playing. My baby girl had just started walking, so I was outside with them.

I was tending to the children, and my boyfriend's male cousin approached me and asked me if he could have twenty-five cents. I remember saying "No, I don't have any money." I said, "You have a wife or girlfriend. Whatever you want, you need to ask her." I don't know what happened, but after that he dismissed himself from me and went back over to my boyfriend and friends. All of a sudden, my boyfriend comes to me like something was on him, and it seemed he was very disoriented and upset. He hit me in my face and punched me in my ear. When he punched me, my ear went silent. It had a ring to it, and I fell down and asked him why he hit me. He stated, "My cousin asked you for some money, so you give my cousin some money. You don't say you have none to give him. You will give him what he asks for."

He started hitting me and hitting me, and no one helped me. Everyone was just standing around. I called the police, but it took them a little bit to get there. I was holding my babies and they were crying, and the police finally came up and asked what happened. My boyfriend told them nothing happened; it was just a small misunderstanding. My boyfriend said, "Right, Tonya? It was just a misunderstanding."

But he hit me. There can't be a misunderstanding about him hitting me. The officer said, "Well, what do you want me to do?" "What are you supposed to do? I never been in this situation before."

My boyfriend looked at me from the other side and said, "We are going to be okay, officer." So I thought that I would be okay, and the days went by, and he started hitting me for no reason.

So I found myself having to fight. He would hit me in my nose, and my nose would bleed. He was hitting me and doing things to me that, if the walls could talk, they would tell it all and the person would stand in awe. The police were called, and they would come out and say, "We can arrest him, but we don't know what will happen after that, and you will have to leave at the time." See, I had nowhere for myself and my children to go, and that hurt. I had no one, nobody to count on, so I would just tell myself that it was going to be okay. I kept telling myself, "I will be okay. I, too, will make it through, just do what he tells you, and you will live through it and then he will soon stop. Just stop fighting him back and take what comes, and you will make it through it all."

One night he came in smelling of alcohol; he was not acting himself, and he walked up to me and pushed me on the bed. He said, "I want you to do some things to me that I feel you need to do." I said, "No, I will not." I told him I needed to go to sleep, and he punched me again in my face, and he ripped my gown off and proceeded to force himself on me. I was screaming and crying, while he punched and kicked me the whole time, choking me and doing things to me that you just can't imagine. I did not get any sleep that night.

His mother would watch the children during the days we worked. One thing about it was she would never whip them, and she took very good care of them, and they would always be happy when I came home. That helped me out a lot. I would always take them to the side and ask them, "If anyone did anything to you… if you have been touched, tell me now." They would tell me, "No, momma." I just felt as a mother I couldn't help myself, but I would do all I could to help them.

I would go to work, and I remember my friends asking me if I was okay. They would say, "You have a look on your face, and I am worried about you." I said, "I will be okay." That is what I always told myself in order to make it through. *Tonya, you have to be okay. This man loves you.* That is what I was fooling myself to believe.

I would tell myself, *See, he doesn't hurt you all the time now, and you and the children have a place to stay. You will be okay.* As the days went by, I was not okay, and the hits kept coming and coming, harder and harder than before. He would force himself on me, and the drinking got worse. I remember one time going to the hospital to see the doctor because I was hurting where I could barely walk, and the doctor came into the room asked me a question. The doctor said, "I have some concerns about your private area, because it is torn really bad right now." I told the doctor I would be fine.

We went home, and my boyfriend grabbed my arm and said, "You will not tell anyone what goes on with us in this house." The police would always get called out, and I would always tell them I would be fine, but I would end up with bruises, headaches, and scratches, and I was getting tired. They did not arrest him without me saying okay, and I could not because he would threaten me. I wondered how I let myself get this far into something I couldn't get out of, and I felt no one could save me from him.

Thoughts from my head

"Lord I should have given up and committed suicide I should have killed my self after all that I went through God your blood came in and covered me even when I felt all alone and felt like no one understood me and no one was there my gentle savior you did not pass me by you were there to hear my humble cry. The tears you caught and the night you protected me while I was in fear you ask me to do something and I will abide in your word. A time is yet for a season and a season I will go through just like you did on the cross."

The Big Move

We were staying with his mom, and he went to jail one day after assaulting me, and again I had to go down and drop the charges. He came home and sat down with me and promised me that it would all stop, and we would start over and move out on our own. He said staying with his mother may have a great impact on our relationship, and I agreed to that, not knowing that things were about to get worse. The hitting had been increasing daily, and struggling to fight was all I knew. Then he started taking my money and doing things that were not like him, and I was getting tired and more scared of him, and growing weaker by the day, but I kept going because I had to fight in order to survive.

I recall one day having to run and hide from him because he had been hitting me, and it hurt so bad that I would have rather just lie down and died. But I heard one of my babies cry out, and that brought me back to knowing I had to fight back, and that is exactly what I did. I said to myself, "It is not over, and I must fight to the finish. He will not take me down. I will not let him. I am tired now. Enough is enough, and this I cannot bear."

I remember running and running one night with my babies down a street trying to get away, and hearing him looking for me as we were running. I was hiding my babies in the bushes and saying, "Don't cry." I started crying out to God to help me and my babies. I ran to my friend's house. "He hit me," I said to her.

"He just kept beating me." My nose and lips were bleeding, and there was blood running down my face. My friend said to me, "You are going to have to get some help or he will kill you." The next thing we heard was a great boom at her door. I said, "He found me. He found us. What do I do? He will hurt me!"

Then he started kicking her door, trying to kick it down. She told him she would call the police, but he did not leave. He stopped after a while and sat down on her porch, and we could hear him cry. He cried so loud and I could hear him say, "I am so sorry Tonya. I promise I won't hit or hurt you again. I will get help. I won't hit you no more. I am sorry." These were the words I heard him say outside the door as he was crying "come back, come back home Tonya come back to me, I love you."

As a young woman, I took what he was saying outside the door and ran with it, meaning I believed what he was saying. All I heard was he would get help and he won't hit me ever again, plus, I did care for this man because he loved me. He said he did, and he was with me all the time, so I knew he was not anywhere else with anyone else.

Finally we went home. Weeks went by, and he did not hit me anymore, just like he promised. I began receiving food stamp benefits because I was not making enough at the school district, and he had gotten fired because of what was occurring between us. I needed to make sure that my babies were able to eat and not have to worry about them going hungry, and I knew that it was only a temporary fix. One weekend I was going shopping to get some things for the babies. I remember where we lived there were bars all along the duplex, so you needed a key to get out of both gates. The front, back, and the windows were hard to exit out of, and I was asleep and did not hear him go out. I woke to find out that he was gone, and I heard the babies playing and laughing in their room, so I got up to dress them so we could go and get some food to eat. I noticed my purse was opened and things were scattered about. My wallet was open and the food stamps were gone, and the little money that I had was gone as well. I tried to get to the door and noticed that my keys were gone also, and my boyfriend had placed a pad lock on the door where he had locked us in so I could not go anywhere. He came back later that day drunk, and it started all over again—the forcing himself on me and beating me, and I just could not take it anymore. I said to myself *I might as well kill myself in order to get out of this mess.* But I had my children, my babies. I couldn't do that to them. I cried out to God, "Please, if you hear me, please help me."

My mother was not close to me, so I had no one that I could talk to. The next week I went to work and told my friends at work I wanted to leave. I starting gathering my belongings and decided I would move my things out little by little so he would not know. I started first gathering the children's clothes and toys and then I would pack my items a little at a time. I went back to work and mapped out a plan with my friends. I couldn't pack anything, because he would know that I was leaving. My friends said, "You can come and stay with me. He will not come to my house. We will help you get on some assistance."

I tried to be as quiet as I could. I did everything he wanted me to do, and it was getting close to the weekend. We got up, and he was leaving, and I made sure I was up to get the kids ready when he left. He left, and I made sure he was gone. Then I gathered my babies, and we walked to the store to use the pay phone, because there was no phone at home.

What I needed for my children was that they as well as I could finally feel safe. So I made the call to my best friend who I work with at the Fort Worth ISD to tell her that we are ready to leave, he is gone the guy I was living with so please hurry and come get us we will be waiting at the house. My friend came as quickly as she could to pick up my kids and I, and we loaded the car with as much as we could take and needed, because we were not coming back to this place of horror and torment. No more will I be locked in the house with the lock on the outside door, nor will I be abused on a daily basis with you forcing yourself on me when you are drunk, and nor will I feel your fist upside my head and face while you are kicking me in the stomach and back because I will be free and my children and I will be safe.

My friend took us to her house located on the military base of Fort Worth, and there we were to remain so I thought until I was able to get back on my feet. Oh, but late that night when all was calm and we were resting, a knock came at the door. The man that I had escaped from was at the door and forcing himself in, and he was not alone. He had several people with him, and he had a gun. The children were in the house, and I did not want anyone to come to any harm. My friend said, "Don't go. I can get the guard. Someone will come and help us, just let me help you." She begged me not to go, but I told her I must go because I did not want anyone to get hurt. I was so scared.

He put a gun to my head and said, "Let's go. Get your things now and I want hurt you or kill you all." So I left my friend's house with my babies, and we went back home with him. Yes, the beatings, the alcohol, the physical abuse was greater than ever. Every day there were weird friends coming by. It never stopped, and come to find out, drugs played a great factor in it all as well. I was tired, and I called the police because once again there goes my head into a wall, my ear punched to where I would hear nothing but silence, and the fight began again with him choking, hitting and kicking me in front of people and they just sit and watch. They arrested him, but he was not there for long before he was released. I pondered in my heart what do I do again, do I sit here and take the abuse or do I fight until I win. So as the days went by and I continued to go on this long journey of pain I had to have more time to come up with a plan. This plan had to be done correctly with no mistakes this time, because if I make one flaw, he will try his best to kill me this time. There was no love in this house only a house filled with pain, and I did not want to continue to live in bitter and shame. I wanted to protect my children and keep them away from the danger that lived close to us everyday in a house filled with so much hate and pain.

In order to protect my children I must flee to somewhere safe where he will never find us again, I will have to stand strong and tall and fight hard to win. Can't say where we will go or what I will do, but I still had my job and friends that were so true.

Now the time had came once again and all I remember is God please help me to overcome my fears. The fear I had inside was the fear of not leaving because I was ready to set out and be safe and on my own, it was the fear that he would find me and do what he said he would do. To have a man who was stronger than you, fight you, steal from you, take all you have and even when you did not want sex, he took your body too. This was a man I can no longer be afraid of, I will just have to step up, be strong and walk away and know that the God whom I had been talking to praying to would hear me and hear me very soon.

Wow God heard me, or was I stepping out to soon because I found a place with very little money in my pocket but I needed somewhere for my children and I to be happy and safe. I was able to put a small deposit on a house off of Rosedale on the east side of town a place for me and the children although it may not have been the best, but it was a place that we could say we can be safe. Safe from the one who I knew was doing so much harm to me, and I just knew my life would be ending real soon if I did not leave. The house had bars around it and I knew that this was what I needed to keep anyone who tried to get in out, and not have to be afraid at night when I closed my eye to go to sleep. I felt when I leave maybe this one time he would give up and let me go my way, or so I thought this man had some plans of his own, and I would never be able to get away even when I thought

I could.

I remember calling my momma and saying, "I have no lights and no food and I am scared. I want to come stay with you mom I am very scared." She came to get me and the kids and took us to get some food and some candles. My mom took us back to the dark house with no lights and told me, "I have a boyfriend, and you cannot stay with me. You have to make it on your own." That is when I knew that I did not have anyone. I was scared and alone with my babies in the dark with fear and harm lurking around, and it felt like death was trying to creep in.

Thinking that the bars would keep anyone from trying to get in but if you want something or somebody so bad you will do anything to make it pass whatever is trying to hold you back. He came later on in the early morning as my children and I slept. He entered in through the back door because the door would not lock because it needed to be fixed, but the bars so I thought were locked safe and secure. He made his way in and would not leave, and I was so afraid. As he proceeded in and startled me he began to say vulgar words at a tone that would scare a woman walking down the street in the dark, fighting and choking me. If I could just get away from this man while he was hitting me, I could get help somewhere because I was tired and I wanted out but had no help. *Oh God, since I can't then let me just die go ahead and kill me, and maybe someone will take care of my babies,* I was saying to myself. I took a piece of glass that I broke by smashing my arm through the window and cut my wrist, and I still have the scars. Although it has healed, it is a reminder of my past.

I was cutting my wrist, and I heard him yelling and screaming. I don't remember too much more, just seeing blood everywhere and going to the hospital. After a while it seemed like another day I was in the hospital, and I had surgery on my wrist. Before I was released, the staff came in to ask what happened. That's when my friends came in and helped me so I would not have to be in this alone.

I was tired, and I called the police and this time I did not drop the charges, I wanted him to be gone out of my life for good. They did arrest him, but he was not there for long before he got released. When he got out, he found out I was gone, and I was *not* coming back. I finally left again. My friends were still by my side, and they helped us.

Words He Said to Me

I will build you a castle with a tower so high that it reaches the moon both day and night.

I would sing a melody sweeter than the birds that fly

I will compose you a tune, and if that doesn't do, I'll try something new

I would take you away with me, as far as I can

To Venus or even Mars or even go to planet Jupiter and we would dine at the Milky Way until our hearts are content with the sweet aroma of love which heaven has sent

That is what I would hear when he spoke to me, something so sweet that it would knock me straight off my feet

I will love you and I will honor you, this is what he said before God and witness to me

But what happened, this was all lies I see no truth you see

I'd boast about you, and I'd be loud, so he said

But quiet I was to everyone else; they did not even have a clue everything you did was all fake and not true. To what was really going on I myself did not know

I will work and I will fight for you the man said to me, work he did but fight was between you and me

A fight to the finish with me it was because this is what you started doing every day a fight you said till the end until one of us stray

We'll make our beds in the clouds, and if that doesn't't do, you told me I'll try something new

So these were the words that a man once told me, and look what happened and where it took me

These are the words I heard a man once say to me, short and to the point in the end really hurt me. Did he really mean what he said, or was it really just words he said to me

The Night that Changed Everything

I went to public housing with the help of my friends and filled out an application, not letting the man I ran from who was abusive to me know that I was about to make the big move. I was accepted for the apartment, and paid the $35 deposit and signed all the papers. The apartment was big and very nice, and I was excited. I told my friends and they were overwhelmed with joy knowing that I would finally be out on my own and free from the hands that tortured me. Yes, everyone was quite happy. My friend's brother would provide transportation for the kids and me to get to daycare and work, then someone would come and get us—not the same person all the time just in case he was watching—and then the babies and I would go to my girlfriend's house and enter at the back so no one could see us. We did this until my apartment was ready for move-in and I would be safe.

I met a friend at work. He was a Chaplain, and I started speaking with him as we sat in the break room and talked about my concerns. I was seeking some advice to help me move and transition into a new start with my children. He also would help us get back and forth to our points of destination safely. We ended up getting as close as friends, but it was nothing more than that, and he was a big help to us. I finally got the key to my apartment, and I was so excited about the great move towards our new life, a new place for us to reside and be free. My friends all gathered around, and we started to do the big move in, and the babies were running around outside, and I would try to keep them in eyesight. I remember I was going to put them in the apartment, but instead I put them in the car so I could make sure I could finish up what was needed so they could go in the house and rest.

Little did I know, my ex-boyfriend found out where I was living and he was in my apartment! I was out gathering some more items and one of the ladies helping me went into the apartment, and he thought it was me. Suddenly, I heard her screaming and saw him running out of the apartment. Someone said to call 911. He ran out, and the police came and gathered what information they could and went looking for him. They were gone for what seemed like a long time, and when they came back they had not found him. They were looking for him, and the ones who were on foot were out of breath and saying to me, "Ma'am, we can't catch him. Now we will give you a report number. We see that you have a great deal of assault charges on him and you have been going through some things." I had about ten or more assault charges on him. They took time out to ask me questions, and after they finished they gave me numbers to certain places and the shelters. I told him I could not go back there because he would find me. I was dropped off at a 7-11, which was a designated drop-off point, and an advocate picked my children and me up and took us to what was supposed to be a secret safe place, and no one was to know where we were. But he did.

I recall going to my mother's house and telling her that he hits me, and I knew that I could not stay there with her because he threatened to harm her too. This was prior to me going to stay with my girlfriend on the base; it was a shelter for battered and abused women and children. I was tired of running, putting my babies in the bushes.

This had been a long journey. The police told me off record, "We are going to tell you what to do, and you will do what is in the best interest for you and your children to protect yourself according to the law. You will abide by the law, and the law will protect you. You will need to make sure that you have people and some protection legally around you when needed. Maybe you can go and seek classes for a gun, but do it the correct way. We cannot tell you what to do with the gun, but you need something for your protection since you are alone with your children."

I kept telling myself I didn't want a gun. I called my mom, and I bought a 45 pearl handle. I went over to my mom's house and told her, "I don't want this." I laid it on her table and told her, "They told me to get it." She was telling me to take the gun and keep it with me at all times and use if I had to, no matter what. Everyone was helping me, and I finally moved into my new apartment, and the clergyman made sure the children and I, were not left alone. We talked with the neighbors and told them a little of what was occurring. I did not have a phone, so if I needed something I was to beat on their wall, which was adjacent to their bedroom, and they would call 911. My friend's brother taught me how to shoot the gun, even though I really didn't want it. The Chaplain told me he would stay with me for a couple of days until we were okay. We were close friends, and he helped me find myself and God once again. The Chaplain had a pager, and if he was needed he would have to go to the hospital if his pager went off. He would always get calls during the day and not at night, but if he did he would always find the time to come back and check on the kids and me. He would make sure we were okay, going to and from work and the daycare, and other places if needed.

The Night I Will Never Forget

It was October 4, 1990, the night of my birthday, and I was in my apartment and loving it with my children. I had just gotten off of work and picked up the children and got them something to eat. I put them down for the night, and I laid on the couch right next to them. It was a small couch, and I also had a giant pallet on the floor for the children. I had my baby girl in my arms and my boys next to us right by me, the Chaplain was on the other side of the room on his pallet, and he received a page. It was late at night. I can't recall the time, but it was very late and raining real hard. He said, "The hospital must need me," and asked if I would be okay until he came back. I said, "I will be okay."

He said, "If anything happens, I need you to take the gun that you purchased and keep it by you for safety. Keep it on safety now, but if by chance anything happens, remove the safety button and use it. Do you hear me, Tonya?" I said okay. So he left and it was not that long of a time before I heard a big kick at my door.

It scared me so bad that I ran and put my baby girl between my boys and pushed them in a corner. I kept hearing this kick, and I forgot about the gun at first. I heard the one man that I thought I had escaped and abused me at the front door saying,

"I am coming to get you, Tonya. I am coming in so just let me in now. I am coming to get you."

I remember I went to the wall and started beating on the wall and thinking if I could just make it to the window in the back, I could run to a neighbor's house. I knew my babies would be okay if I could just get the police out here.

I went to the window in the back of one of the bedrooms, and there was a man standing at the window. I was afraid and scared for my children. I ran back to the front, and I thought about the gun; as soon as I retrieved it, I took it off safety, and as soon as I did the front door came open, I saw him. He had gone the other way because I had left a light on the stove in the kitchen just enough for me to see, but not anyone if they ever came in. He came to where I was standing in the middle of the floor. I ran in the room where my babies were so I could protect them. He approached me and said, "I will kill you. You were not to leave me, and you are coming back home." I heard others coming in, and before I knew it, the gun went off and I had shot him. The gun went off several times, and he was still coming toward me.

I realized what had happened and threw the gun out the front door. He was still coming toward me. We were right at the front door almost, and he was looking at me. Then all I heard was him saying, "You shot me. Why did you shoot me?" Blood was coming down everywhere, all on the floor, and he was yelling, "She shot me!" I heard screaming outside the door and cars sounding like they were racing away. The blood was pouring on the floor and sounded like a water faucet. He was trying to grab me, and I was trying to get out the door. People were coming outside yelling, "What's going on?" and somebody said, "Call 911."

I don't even know what happened to the gun. When the police tried to find the gun they could not even find it. It was gone. I remember hearing sirens, and he sat down on the concrete and cried and told me he was sorry. Someone went in my house and got my babies and took them to the next-door neighbor's house for safety. I watched him and told him that I was sorry: I did not mean it. I watched him dying right before my eyes, and he was crying and yelling. I was hysterical and crying. I could hear all the sirens and see the helicopter lights shining down. The one officer approached me yelling and screaming at me. My sister worked for the police department, and one of the officers knew me and knew my sister, so he stated, "I got this." He told the other officer to call downtown to get my sister, who was working dispatch. They told me that my babies were okay.

He was still lying down, and a man approached me and said he was a detective and he needed to go into the house. "We are going to take you into the house where your babies are to have a seat, and they can see you; they are crying." They covered my ex-boyfriend up and took me into the neighbor's house. I remember someone said to me, "We have to go," and I said, "I am not going to jail. I don't want to get in the car. I did nothing wrong." The policeman said, "You are not going to jail. We just need a statement from you as to what happened. It looked like self-defense, we promise you."

We went downtown and entered the room, and seeing my name and his name deceased on a board caused more tears to run down my face. I was cold and wet; I had someone's jacket on. I don't know how long we stayed, but I felt as though my life was destroyed and cut into many little pieces. I remember going to my sister's house afterward; it was a place no one knew, and at that time I called his mother and said I was sorry, and I heard the family in the background telling me they were going to kill me. I remember having nightmares like they were real; it felt as if he was in my presence, and he was coming to kill me. I did not receive counseling because I felt I could push all my problems to the back of my mind and hide them and not worry about anyone asking why did you stay, or why did you allow this to go on so long; and plus it hurt me a great deal, and I was not the same anymore after this. I did care for him, and I did not want to hurt him or kill him like he had done to me the whole time we were together. He killed me a long time ago.

I was evicted from my apartment. They said even though it was not my fault, I could not have weapons or violence while on housing. I remember the D.A. telling me that this was not my fault. They said, "Little did you know, they were coming to kill you. They had already planned to kill you. They had someone call your mom and tell her that you were already dead." My mom did not know where I was; she had never been over to my new place. Someone called her and told her I was dead, and she was scared. The other guys did not get caught, and it is unclear who they were. No one from the family was to talk to me or contact me or they would get arrested because of the threats. I did not seek help, and it took a toll on my life throughout the many years I tried to block it out of my mind. I do know now that I probably should have, because it took me down a path that caused more pain. I would always try to tell myself that greater is He and He alone is in me, so God you help me to overcome these obstacles. God, please help me, Jesus. All I would say is help me, God, please help me. I would recite these words to myself every day.

> The Lord is my shepherd I shall not want.
> He maketh me to lie down in green pastures;
> he leadeth me beside the still waters.
> He restoreth my soul. He leadeth me in the
> paths of righteousness for his names sake.
> Yea though I walk through the valley of the shadow of death
> I will fear no evil for thou art with me. Thy
> rod and thy staff they comfort me.
> Thou prepares a table before me in the presence of
> mine enemies. Thou anointes my head with
> Oil. My cup runneth over.
> Surely goodness and mercy shall follow me all the
> days of my life, and I will dwell in the house
> of the Lord forever and ever. PSALMS 23: 1-6 KJV
> Amen

I love these words. I kept saying, "God, you please help me and my babies. God, you please help me, because I can't get past this situation and I don't have anybody." I had to find somewhere to stay for me and the children because we couldn't stay with my sister. She had my niece and her house was only big enough for them, and plus we didn't see eye to eye, but I did love her a lot. She would love me for a little bit, and talk to me for a while, and when that would stop I would force myself on to her to get that love. I remember saying one night, *God, if you just let me sleep, help me, and protect me and my children. I know you are there; I can feel your presence unlike before. I know you are there; you helped me to make it out for a reason. I don't know what it is, God, but please help me. I don't know what the reason is, but please help me to know what it is and take care of us, and if I keep it in your hands, we will be all right.*

I recall trying to fall asleep and my dad saying, "I will help you find you a place to stay." I was still working at the bus barn, but at that time I was off. I still had the support of my friends by my side. I found a new place, and my dad paid the deposit for us to move in. This was a new chapter in my life, but in the back of my mind I was still fighting what I had just gone through, and it was devastating to me. I thank my sister for being by my side, for letting us live with her for a while and coming to my aid to make sure that the children went to school daily. I did not have a car, but my dad finally was a great help to me and provided me a car. It was good enough to get me from point A to point B, and that is all I needed.

Women Don't Give Up

Thoughts of a Woman

There are some things in my life that I had to go through and did not understand why they were allowed. Lord, please help me to overcome. Help me with my fears and to go through my trials, dear God. Your will is what I have to accept, and now I understand why the toils and trials of this life have taken me to another level that I never knew existed. I have been through many trials and dangers in my life, and by the grace of God I have made it through. His grace and mercy has followed me throughout this long journey in my life.

I am still young and have many more hills to climb, but with God on my side I will not fail. Though the scars have been healed by cream and bandages, God's love I will still remember. Yet, I will not forget that it reminds me that I have Jesus who has brought me through the rugged terrains, and though once scorned and broken, now I am healed.

The winds blew and the storms came hard. I watched the leaves blow off the branches and a small tornado rip the house, shredding it to tiny pieces. I saw myself sometimes going down just like that tree when the storm hit. But oh how I made it by God's mercy and his wonderful grace.

Life throws a stumbling block in your way, but you have to stand tall, strong, and firm to what it is and watch the change occur. If you give it all to God and know that He will never leave you nor forsake you, He will be there till the bitter sweet end.

I am a woman who has been hurt, battered, beaten, and bruised, sometimes to the point where I just wanted to give up, but I made it. Yes, Tonya Michelle made it through the storms that were raging in her life both day and night. I had to say, God, I know you see what I'm going through. When will it all end? When will my life begin?

I heard Him call my name one day, and I had to answer. I am glad that I did because now I feel so free. Free from the pain, the guilt, the sorrow, free from being hurt, free from the beating, and free from being scorned.

To all you ladies feeling the abuse, the neglect, and ridicule, hold your head up and know that God is on your side, standing next to you to carry you all the way. He will never leave you nor forsake you, so give it to him and put your head on the pillow and go to sleep knowing that God has it all under control.

Let go and let God fix it, and after a while you won't have to struggle, cry, feel lonely, depressed, sad, or even miserable, because He will bring sunshine to your life, and rainbows will follow thereafter.

So, women, I say don't give up and don't fear, because trouble lasts but a small season; joy will come in the morning and the pain will leave. The scars remain, but as long as you have Jesus you don't have to worry about a thing. Nor will you fall. Give it all to the Lord and stand still, tall, and firm and watch what He can do for you.

I'm Gonna Hold On

I'm gonna hold on
No matter what comes my way
I'm gonna hold on

Satan can't knock me down
You can't stop me regardless of what you do
Trying to knock me, talk about me, hurt
me, or even do harm to me

I'm gonna hold on

So whatever comes my way
I'm gonna hold on
Yes from day to day
I'm gonna hold on

Holding on to God, my faith I will keep, my trust
I have so please watch over me as I sleep
I'm gonna hold on

Trusting in His word, reading even His word day by
day, I will hold on no matter what comes my way
He said he would never leave me, so I'm
building my trust and faith in Him

I'm gonna hold on

When you see me standing tall, as short as I am, no matter
what you know about me, life is not always so grand.
I'm gonna hold on

Even if you can't stand me, hate me, and even despise
me, my God will not let me fall because He has me
I'm gonna hold on
Even though you try, I am his child and God is
with me day by day walking by my side
I'm gonna hold on

He will see me through, surrounding me with his loving
arms of protection while the angels protect me too
If you choose otherwise and don't want to go, just
know I have to go on, and I must let go, trusting in
his word and knowing he will see me through

That's why I'm gonna hold on
Yes God I'm gonna hold on to you

I am grateful

In all that I have been through, I am still grateful. I am grateful to even be here, because God could have taken me when the devil was strongly in my life, but God surrounded me and protected me with his precious mercy and grace. So I will walk into my purpose for what He has for me to do while I have the blood still running through my veins.

It is so good to be grateful and know that God will always bless you regardless of who wants to or even those who do not want you to be blessed. So I will continue to keep praising Him and worshiping Him, and God will open up all the mysteries that He has for me.

Being grateful, I will give you all the glory honor and praise for what you have done. I know that the secrets that God has will be revealed to me and He will show me what to do—my purpose that I am here for.

I am grateful that I still have my life, health, and strength because of the surgeries that I have been through, and by the grace of God I made it through. I should never have made it through two of them. God has moved me from different places and different people because He said, *I have chosen you, and I need you to go through this, my child.* So I now am very thirsty for what he has for me, and all that is for me I will do. This came because of the gratefulness that I have for Him, and I see now that I have been touched with what He has and what He can do for me and where He has put me. See, I was not worthy to be here, and so I know I have to give Him all the praises and be very thankful for all that He has.

I am grateful because He has opened doors for me and has shielded me from all hurt, harm, and danger. I need him all the time, because without Him I will lose my mind.

I am truly grateful for my children and grandchildren, knowing that I can teach them about a man who can supply and take care of all their needs. I see them praising him and speaking about Him now at their tender young ages. They tug me while we are in church, saying, "Mimi I want more of God." It brings a smile to my face.

Worship is what I was told is like therapy to me, and when I feel like I am losing my mind, God takes all the problems I have and puts them in a pile and blows on them and it comes out for the good. God is good, and He is good all the time.

So being grateful is so good to my soul, knowing that God has a plan for me, and I will rise up, step up to the plate, and walk in what He has for me.

"Woman, thou art loosed from thine infirmity." Luke 13:12 KJV

So don't dwell on your infirmity. Be grateful for what is, give it all to Him, and let Him use you in whatever He has. Talk to Him and hear what He has to say. Let Him come in you and fill you and see what He can do in you. See how you can become just like him. He knows all that you are and has given you things that must come to your knowledge, so grab onto the Lord and learn of Him so you will know what He wants from you. If you are going through something, Jesus will lay His hands on you, and you will feel joy, and you will come out learning what he wants you to know. Learn yourself and get into the presence of God and ask Him to help you, and watch and see how quickly

God can change you.

But the hour cometh, and now is, when the true worshipers shall worship the Father in spirit and in truth; for the Father seeketh such to worship him.

John 4:24 KJV

Be ye grateful unto God, and He will help you in all that it is for you. He will give you the desires of your heart only if you believe I say to all women.

I am so grateful my father, for I know now that you are and have been there for me. Thank you, Father, for where you are about to lead me. I don't know, but you will give it to me in increments, and I will enjoy knowing what it is to need you, Father, tell me just what I need to do. I don't need anyone to tell me, just you. I will praise you and give you all the glory and honor, for I will keep on talking to you until I hear from you and you reveal the desire you have for me. I will continue being a faithful servant for you and go out and tell each woman, man, and child that if they seek you and give you the praise, they will be healed.

I don't want anyone to think that they can take that praise from me, because it is embedded in my soul and I will store it there until I die. You know me as a woman, and you know all my desires and the times that I do wrong. Help me to enter into your kingdom and help me to change. I will give you all glory and all the praise because you called me to you and I ran until I fell down and worshiped you. I am healed from all that I have been through, and I know you are here with me forever. God, I will keep on reaching for you. I will lift my eyes to you. I am very grateful now and forever more. I hear you saying, *The knowledge is here for you, and I will grab on and hold on to it.*

But whosoever drinketh of the water that I shall give him shall never thirst; but be in him a well of water springing up into everlasting life.

John 4:14 KJV

I am grateful for no more depression, no more abuse, no more being twisted. Grateful for being able to worship you. Grateful for the sickness and for now not having the low self-esteem that I used to have. I will run after you and search for you until I know I have you. I need you in my life so that I will let every woman who has had doubt and had a broken heart find you and know you are there and will heal and mend. All hope is in you, and I surrender all of myself to thee.

Amen, Amen, Amen

I Am Healed

I am healed, and I truly know because I no longer feel the same as I used to. I no longer walk in the ways that I used to or think like I used to.

God has healed my mind and my body and given me a new way to go. Trusting is what I do now, so I do know that I can press on to higher things that the Lord has for me.

Healed having faith, enduring till the end, accepting what God has for me, learning to lean and depend on the master, everlasting life is what God promised to me and delivering me from all my sin that I no longer do anymore.

See, all I ever needed was a great touch from the master above who took all the wrong that I did and made it right for me. I got down on my knees and asked, *Please, Father, I am here in need of prayer and calling on your name. Please come see about me. Pull me through, and I promise I will take hold of your hand and grab on and let you have control.*

Bless me, Father, and heal me. I promise I will change and won't go back. New life I will make, because you are there for me and will hold on to me. No more worrying, feeling doubtful, healed from my pain, and the pain that I did to myself as well as I let others do to me, if and when I allowed it. Gone from the hurt and the pain so that I will not be done wrong anymore and will stand up and press on to a new and better way of life.

I have given it to the master and pressed forward and the Lord has truly healed me to do his will. Walking in the right path is what I long for and never to turn around, because I one day would like to see the doctor who has truly healed me.

This Place

Once upon a time, I was afraid and discouraged woman, a woman who thought that she would never be able to take care of herself and her children and would never be anything. *You will never be anything*, I said to myself, *so just settle for what will come your way.* Now I look back over my life and know that I have come too far to turn around knowing that the Lord has been there with me and my children all the time. I thought I was all by myself, but He was always with me, carrying me.

Now I am in a place where no one but God has taken me to. This place that I am in is a great place of peace, comfort, and smooth tranquility. This place that I am currently in is a place where I love to reside each and every day from this day forth. I am living my life so different now, feeling free from pain, misery, and strife. See, in this place I found a great man who takes very good care of me when I am down and feeling hurt deep inside. Without being in this place, I would cry many tears and feel like I just want to leave and never return. In this place I feel free; in this secret place God will cover me from the hurt and harm of what is to come to me. I have seen a lot of things and been a lot of places that I should not have even gone. Places where few should not have ever have had to dwell in. The things that I have been in I can truly say I will no longer be in again, because in this place I am in now I am very happy. My joy, peace, and strength are in this place, and I am living, breathing, and doing well. I let go and gave up and gave it over to God, and he has taken me to a sweet and beautiful place where no one comes in unless I let them. I was quite tired and had very limited options in my life, because I was so hurt and abused and wanted to just die. All the strength I had in me was gone and all my tears were starting to dry up, so I begged and said, God, if you just touch me, I know I will be okay.

Now I am content, full of joy, and happy as ever and not thinking about what will lie in front of me because I know the Lord will speak and it will be so. So in this place I will run to you with open arms, sing my songs, and feel the love that I longed for and looked for from a man. I will continue to give you all the glory, praise, and honor. My heart is now healed, and the scars that once were down my back, side, face, and arms are starting to heal.

I know you belong to me now, and all I have to do in this place is call on you and you will hear me and come to me, sit with me, and speak to me. In this place I see white everywhere, and the garden that I enter is so full of peace; the birds are flying around me and chirping a great tune. In this place I sit on a rock and look around and say, *this is a place where I truly want to be because it is so full of joy and love.* This place is very hard to describe unless you have been here before, and if not one day you to will try your best to seek this place. I never knew my life would feel this way, thinking that I could never get over my past. My heart felt heavy, and the pain hit me like a brick wall. In this place I found Jesus, and in this place I feel free. This is a place where God can use me and will keep me covered. Use me, Lord, empty this vessel take away all the hurt, tears, and pain. I never thought I could ever get over because I've been through so much. I am so amazed to be here a place where I can fall into the arms of Jesus, and He will truly take care of me in this place. Take care of me, oh Lord, I know yes you will truly take care of me in this sweet, oh so sweet place. This place is where I truly want to be; a place full of joy, love, and peace and nobody but Jesus can take me to that secret place.

Worthy to be Praised

Ladies, come on and clap your hands.
No matter what you are going through or
have been through, stomp your feet.
Let's shut the devil out, lifting up our voices crying and singing
out to the Lord. For He is our father and worthy to be praised.
No matter the circumstance, healing will come through our
praise, and we will praise him until we feel a breakthrough.
Shouting onto the Lord, cry out, to the Lord.
Sing out to the Lord.
Give it to the Lord loudly and say even so, it will be
and He is still worthy, our God, to be praised.
Crying out to you in all that I have been through,
hear me, Lord. Help me and bring me out of all
the troubles that are hindering my way.
Mend me, make me, shape me, mold me into what
you have me to be so that I will lift my voice.
And cry out to you to the heavens, I hope to see you soon. My
healing and deliverance I will receive, and pain will go away
and the scars will truly be healed and yes, Lord, I will feel free.
Free from all life's pain, life's trials, and free to be loved
for a lifetime. Free to be who you want me to be, and all
I can say is that you are worthy to be praised. From the
top to the bottom, I will praise you even in advance.

Cuddle me, comfort me, hold me, and rock me. Give me peace, joy, and love, for I will lift my voice and cry out to you. Yes, you are worthy to be praised, and I will praise you until the end.

I Want You to Know

Lord, I want you to know that I love you so. You are a very important part of my life, and I know that I can't do anything without you.

My soul, my relationship with you, Lord, I cherish so deeply. So deeply that nothing and no one can compare.

Prayers I say to you each and every day has helped me to make it all this way. Your love is so very important, so that's why, Lord, I want you to know, oh how I truly want you to know, how much you mean to me.

The love that I hold dear and close in my heart for you, no other can compare. The feelings that I share with others about you, I hold deep within my heart, and no other can compare to how great you have been to me. I love you each and every day, yes because you have shown me and kept me on the straight and narrow way. You have shown me how to love, live, and endure the struggles of this daily life that rest on my shoulders each and every day. The trials that come to me even in the middle of the night you have shown me how to make it through, so I will put all my trust, Lord, in you.

I fall down on my knees, and as I close my eyes I think back and reflect on all that has passed me by. The lonely nights, those sleepless night, and nights filled with so much pain that I thought that I would not make it through. Oh, how your tender loving mercy and grace, which has been with me all the way, helped me to survive another day.

Lord, I want you to know that I love you so, and I will keep you in my heart and in my mind. My soul, Lord, belongs to you and no other, and you are truly all I need to get by. Yes, this is a small confession that I hold so dear in my heart, and I just want you to know I love you so.

Without you, Lord, I can't make it through all my heartaches and my pain. When mountains seem too high, and the valley too low and all the rivers too wide for me to cross, I know I can call on your name and you'll be there to help me through it all. That's why I want you to know that I truly do love you.

You have guided me on my way each and every day. Though your guidance, wisdom, and strength, Lord, I stayed strong with my head held high. Your love is everywhere, and that is what helped me as I traveled through life's long journey that is filled with sometimes good and sometime bad. But through it all you held me so tight in the palm of your hand.

So that's why, Lord, I want you to know that yes, I did walk through the valley and shadows of death and knew that even though I sometimes feared evil, you, Lord, was always there right by my side, never leaving me alone.

I just want you to know that through it all, I love you so. Sometimes I may slide down, and I even may fall; I may also bounce my head on the wall. I may have left you, but I know you never left me, and you always held your hand out to me. I do not show you often enough that I appreciate and care, but yes, Lord, I just want you to know I do love you. Whether the blessing you bless me with be big or small, I will still love you through it all. I know I don't deserve all that you do and have done for me, but I truly thank you, Lord, for sparing me. I do love you so. Even if I never get another blessing from you, Lord, you have already done enough.

So I say hold on and enjoy the ride that God has put you on and let him be the driver, and you surely will not ago wrong. Buckle up and don't fight whatever may come your way; just know that the Lord always has it in the palm of his unchanging hand.

So I just want you to know that I do love you, Lord, I do love you so.

No Separation of Love

Poem
It would be easier to take the wet from water
or take dry from sand than for anyone to try to separate us
or stop us from holding hands.
Because I love you, see I love you from the bottom of my heart,
and what love has joined together can't nobody take it apart.
It would be easier to take the cold from
snow or take the heart from fire
than for anyone to take my love from you,
because you're my heart's desire.
And I love you, really do love you. I love
you from the bottom of my heart.
And what love has joined together, can't nobody take it apart.
Lord, you are mine day after day;
Cheering for you is what I long to do
best in each and every way.
Patient, tender, smiling, true always ready for you
Faltering courage and to share all the
day of my many cares for you
Dreaming dreams are all I long for
Brighter years will come, pleasure is what I will have,
knowing that you will always be here in my life for me
Lord of mine, we've shed some tears together, and you
were there to catch each and every one for me
With the passing of the many years and all of the many
fears, somehow you've always made a way for me

I always said to myself that I could bear the blows that
hit me even so hard and stand up straight and tall,
but each and every time they hit, I would just fall
You smiled on me to show me just how brave I truly could be,
and I keep my faith in you all the way
Lord of mine, with more years to come and the
promises I made to you, I did not ever want to break
Knowing how luxuries and costly things come
and grow old with time, the many gowns of
silk and not having desires for wine
Jeweled rings and the nice, beautiful things
You will be there for me, as you are truly
worth more than any silver and gold
So you bless me, Lord, and I will truly be satisfied. If it
came Fed X or even in a brown paper bag, and what love
put together, no one can take apart to make us sad
One day my dreams will truly come true, and I will have all
that my heart so desires by your wonderful mercy and grace.
I too will meet and greet you in the sky
You are my child, come on home, because home
is truly where you need to be and belong.
Welcoming me with eyes that shine of
love and will always is true to me,
Come on, my child, come on in, for this time
you are at the end and you will win.
Love will keep us together whether near or far, and
yes for right now you are truly in my heart.
No separation of one's love is what I see,
and Lord yes, we are a team.

So They Say

You are so wondrous unto my sight, so they say.
The innocence of your virginal delight, so they say.
You desire the passions of this earth.
I give you all I am….I give you all I'm worth.

Entreat me not to leave you; know I will never will, so they say.
But hope that I am near you; this I hope I shall fulfill.
Forever know I am at your side or a
few short steps just behind,
And in you I need reach out, have faith in what you did.

My strong embrace for holding you near, so they say.
My able shoulder for you to shed a tear.
My caring voice for your heart to hear.
My paternal protection to suppress your fear.

Wherever you may be, you must forever know
My heart will never forget you, and
there I'll always go, so they say.
Wherever your life may find you, there I choose to live.
This vow I give only unto you to you so I may I live and give.

In the place that you must pass and know your final breath,
In that very place, my love, I too will
choose my death, so they say.
When that time is upon me, this will be my cry

With true love did I live my life…
with that love I die? So they say.

No a wondrous place full of innocent delight.
Again you appear wondrous unto my sight, so they say.

Touch of Real Love

As the sun touches the summer's sky,
You're constantly on my mind.
When we first met, and I felt that first warm touch,
I knew you were one of a kind.
The natural beauty that I felt stayed on me for a long
time, and I did not want to let it go; it was so genuine.
I felt that I was not worthy to even have you to come
into my life and do just what you said you would do.
The expressive love that came in my heart was
something that I just could not describe.
Lord, your beauty I will one day see and wish that
I would be able to emanate from within me.
You are all I need, and I truly will sit at
your feet to praise your holy name.
A wonderful change has come over me, and I
truly enjoy it and hold on for the long ride.
I need you to stay by my side now because
you bring such love to my world
A love that no one will ever be able
to show without being fake.
That unconditional love that goes beyond the many
Skies above.
Of all that I wish, I wish that everyone could feel the
way that I do, feeling that warm, soft, gentleness that
makes you so real. One day I will go to a peaceful

place never to be known until you have entered in,
and yes your love you truly have shown to me
Now I say that if I should part from you, please keep your hand extended out so that when I return I will hold on and never let go. Your love has been etched in my heart, and the tears that fall from my face are tears of great joy. Lord, I love you, and I will hold on each and every day as long as I shall live, because you have shown me the real way.

Trust

I don't care what people think about me
I sometimes don't care what they say
I don't care what they think of you, Lord
I'm going to ask you to stay
I don't care if they start to avoid me
I don't care what they do
Because I trust you
I have you and know you will never leave
me, for you are always true
I don't care about anything but just being with you Lord
I say to myself, don't go, don't give up, don't leave the scene
I will trust you in spite of what I see or even what I am going through, and especially what I hear, if it is not from you. You, Lord, are my King because all I know is that I am with you, Lord, and you have truly helped guide my steps in each and every way throughout my many days. I had my heart broken and made many mistakes, but I trust you in spite of what they say. Sometimes I feel like I am by myself, but I will trust you, Lord, to show me the way, because knowing that you are there with me, I know that I am never all alone because you are the strength that is beneath my feet.
I've heard a warning voice from friends and close relations saying seek his trust and don't give up. You will be in the comfort and be able to trust him. Just don't give up. So I decided to take that step and heed to the word of advice and it truly paid off.

They told me all about your reputation of
being just who you are—a trusting man.
No other man can compare to you.
So yes, I will think of you first in all that I do, and
if I shall fall I know you will be there to pick me
up and dust me off and place me back in the right
path, and I will stick to you like super glue.
I don't care what they think if I fall and what
they say when they see my mistakes, I will stay
and let you fight all my battles all the way
And yes, I will truly stay and trust in you, for you
are my way maker through and through.

I'll Make It

When my life was tossed and turned, Jesus helped me to make it through the storm as I began to turn.

When it seemed I couldn't be found, he stepped in right on time and picked me up off the ground, and now I am safe and sound. I know that I made it through with just a touch of his unchanging hand and I know that he has a plan for me to make it.

When it seemed like all hope was gone and it seemed like I was all alone and I just could not go on, I threw my hands up and looked toward heaven and knew that I would make it through.

When it felt like I just didn't want to live and I felt like there was nothing I could give, God stepped in right on time, and I made it through the storms on a very small, thin dime.

I believe and know that I will make it without a shadow of a doubt, and I will make it without anyone slowing me down, and I will run on to see what the end will be. Just you, my friends, wait and see.

Run on, my child, run on into his loving arms and give it all, and you will never be in any harm.

When it felt like all hope was gone and it seemed like I just could not make it on my own, I would run just to see what the end would be. Oh, come on, scorned woman, and hang with me.

God stepped into my life in the nick of time, and I made it through, yes, without drinking wine. Yes, I will make it, you see, and that feels great to me, but when I let go of God's hand, I fell way down into a pit of sinking sand, and with a loud cry he heard me and reached his hand out again with open arms, and he pulled me close to him.

I'll hold on to him this time no matter what may come my way, and though the storms may rise, the mountains are high. I have to climb and press my way through, watching and knowing his mercy and his grace will see me through.

Lord, please bring me out of all my misery and pain. Please stop all the rain, because you are my life, my will, my rock, sword, and shield. You will see me through all the valleys and hills. See, it is your will.

Jesus, you have never left me, nor will you ever leave me, no matter how I am, and you will save me, clean me up, and keep me from a growling man. You have never let me down, and of course you will always be around.

Holding me, shaping me, loving me, and providing for me.

You are all I need as a woman who was scorned. I will never have to feel that way ever again because you are the true man who I will always adore who keeps me from all hurt and all harm.

The harm of a man, oh no more, and I will never let you go, because I know I'll make it.

Thank you for the healing

Thank you for the love

I have made it past all that I have been through, even in all the sickness and all the pain, I made it through. The scars are healed and the pain is gone, and I will never, ever let no man do me wrong.

If I should fall that way again, I promise to give it to you, my friend. You are my Lord, and you will see me through because I truly can count on you.

Though trouble and trials may fall, even the tears they fall like rivers of water in the great ravine, I will see you through it all, and you will stand firm and tall.

I'll make it, and yes I will make it through. Scorned but not broken is what you made me.

Jesus, you have never left me and never will you ever forsake me, so ride on, King Jesus, swoop me as you pass by, and I will hop in your car and enjoy the ride. This lets me know I've made it by the grace of God, and with his loving hands I will win and be proud.

Proud to say to all the women of the nation who have and even not have been scorned. Yes, you will make it. Yes, I'll make it through.

Hold on, Child

Hello, God, I know you are a great man because you have taken care of me and brought me out of many of storms. As for me, I have been making it through everyday life by your grace and mercy thus far. It has been hard for me, but I am so grateful that you are by my side all the way, carrying me when times have gotten too hard.

I'm sitting here in this lonely room thinking about all that I have been through and hope that sooner than soon I will be okay too. What I am saying is that when I thought I could not make it, you have told me don't give up. Just give it all to me, and you will see victory in the end. Whatever you are doing, I will try my best to keep my hands out of it and watch the miracles occur.

Lord, if it is too much, all I want you to do is to guide me in all that I am facing. Give me the courage and the wisdom to make it through whatever you are trying to have me to go through. I know you love me, and each and every chance I get I will show that same love back in return to you, because you have done so much for me that I surely cannot tell it all to you. Sometimes I feel like I am coming unraveled at what life has dealt me, and I won't make it through the trials that will come my way. Lord, I know that we will always be together; it will be me who let you go and fall, but no matter what, you will always be there to pull me through.

Lord, you are on my mind every day and night, and I

can't help thinking about you, but sometimes I get filled with depression, loneliness, and hurt. I wonder sometimes how I can truly go on in this hateful world filled with disgust, pain, strife, and misery. But I hear you say to me, *Hold on, my child, don't give up and in time you will see my works. Lean on me, Tonya, and know that everything will be all right. I hold the stars the moon and the skies in the palm of my hand. I am the great I am the one who holds life in the palm of my hand, the one who holds both day and night and life and death. What makes you think I can't take care of your needs? What make you think I will not see you through? Hold on, my child, be strong and in time you will be the head and not the tail a leader and not a follower. I will never leave you nor forsake you see I am the only one that can truly see you through. I am here until the end of time and forever even after when I shall call you on home. Hold on, my child, and see what I have for you.*

    So, Lord, this is what you mean to me if I can truly say

    Your love is giving not taking

    Mending not breaking

    Trusting and believing in your every word

    Patiently hearing from me and listening to all I have to say

    Faithfully sharing each tear and dream

    Each joy and every sorrow today and tomorrow

    Understanding never demanding

    It's your strength never failing despite my changes

    A promise from me to you, a promise that was broken that should have been stuck together like glue. A promise I said that I will never break again for you have showed me the way and I love it every day. Time you gave to me was the time I shared so dear and near my heart. The life you bore for me on that old rugged cross I will cherish it till I am called home and that was your very own life you gave and yes you were even placed in a grave. You rose for me and said you would come back and I truly feel my Lord you will always be the best man truly a great man. So yes, I will hold on and yes, I will do my best to be strong.

Sorry

This is what I wanted a man to say to me, especially the man that I loved who took me through the rough valleys in my life. The man who said that he would never hurt me and would always take care of me, whether it was the man who raised me or the man who married me, and even the man who was supposed to have been there for me. The man who said he would never hit me, lie to me, cheat on me, and, of course, steal from me—the man who I called on, someone who was supposed to have been there for me. The man who said he would shield me from all harm and danger, who would come and protect me. What happened to the vows that you said before God and to me? What happened to that, I just want to know.

You would always say to me, "I'm sorry for the pain I've caused. I'm sorry for not understanding the true value of a wife. I'm sorry for the lonesome nights and for the wrong I've done. I'm learning now just how it feels to lose that special someone when you push them away from you." He would tell me that we had good times that were shared between the both of us, and I know it will follow me wherever I go. He would tell me he thanked God for bringing me into his life, but how so when you hurt me and did not try to help me? No happiness you brought to me, just pain each day.

You know that life has stumbling blocks that you must try

your hardest to overcome. Many of them are like a tall brick wall that you can't break; you have to endure and get over them the best you know how.

Lord, I'm sorry. These were always the words that he said after everything he did to me that was not right.

I'm sorry, can you forgive me? These are the words that always came out of the mouth of the man who said he did care. What did I'm sorry really mean to him when he would only repeat the cycle of wrongness over and over again?

I just pray that on life's highway, I one day will understand, forgive, and let the Lord teach me how to love again and show the love that I truly look for and desire in a man, from when it comes even till the end. For sorry is no more that I will have to endure.

Love

It's love that builds a happy home—the love that you can only get from one place where it is genuine, pure, and perfect. From a man who is so true to all that he does. The love that is so sweet is just like music to my ears. The love that warms my heart and fills me with joy each and every day of my life. See, this love will tell me that I truly belong to him, and he will hold me and cradle me in his arms. This love that I get will help me when times are hard and it feels as though I just can't go on. I even had people in my life that I knew I should not, but I was looking for love in places to fill the void in my life. I searched all over and could not find the true love that I was missing.

It's love from someone who shows gentleness each and every day. It's love that follows every dream and shows you the way to go. Its love that warms the heart and soul that makes me feel whole. The love that will not have you to ponder or even wonder if it is so real, because you can truly feel it when it happens.

I want to introduce you to a man who will give you all the love that you will ever need. The man that I am speaking about is my Lord—your Lord if you allow him to be. The man we call Jesus who bled and died for me and for you. The day that he died was a day filled with more love than one could ever know. You will fill with his love when you accept him into your heart, mind, and soul. Flow love into me, Jesus. From you I will accept and take hold, and I promise with that love I will share to all.

I thank you, Lord, yes I do for all your love that you have given to me because now I can truly feel what true love is. I have experienced bad love, sad love, and no love. That kind of love is the love you want to throw away and leave alone. Take it, bury it so that it can never come again and cut you just like a two-inch sword.

Lord, I love you for the happiness, for all your gentleness you have brought to me, so teach me, and help me to give it to all who pass my way in life. The love that you show through your kindness and your mercy, help me thus this far to make it and many of blessings I know now come from unconditional love from you, Father.

For God so loved the world that he gave his only begotten son. That is the most love that anyone could ever have for us. That is truly the first love, the deepest love, and a very strong love from on high to man down here on earth.

From the first time I accepted you in my heart, I knew there was something very wonderful and special, and I reached out, drew near, accepted it, and allowed it to flow completely. I will love you with my whole heart, and I will stay and fight the battle you put before me, no matter how long it may take and hard it may get. I will never feel that I can't feel your love because it is truly there, so let go and feel what it means to have true love in your life from a man who gives it unconditionally, always and forever.

I searched all over and could not find the true love that I was missing—the love from you, Lord. There is nobody greater than you and nothing greater than your love.

Brighter Day

(Poem)

There is a brighter day when everyone will see the way.
He's coming back real soon, so everyone get ready, get
ready for that day, ready for that day, it is coming real soon.
Yes, he will come for me, and he will come for you.
He's coming like a thief in the night, so you better get
your house in order and get it right. For that day when he
comes is real soon. Coming like a thief in the night, like
the wind roaring through the trees with a great big breeze,
so have your heart right, your thoughts right, and your
mind regulated for what is about to happen real soon.
Get ready for that day when we will be able to see his
sweet face and hear his voice say well done my good
and faithful servant. So let us all get ready for that
day and get ready for it to come to us real soon.
Brighter day for me, a brighter day for you, is what I heard
him say to me. See, he told me that he loves me no matter
what I go through and no matter what I do. No matter what
I have done in the past and even the present, as long as I fall
on my knees, repent, and give it to him and ask for sincere
forgiveness. He will forgive me, and yes there will be a brighter
day coming to me real soon. I will praise his holy name and
be ready for that day that gets bright days to come real soon.
Brighter day is what we will see, and we will rejoice
in his name and praise him forever the more. Just

to seek his wonderful face is what I have been
longing for, and the wait will not be in vain.
The sun will always shine and no more pain, rain, or feeling
the loneliness of no one being there to hold me help me and
tell me that it will all be okay, just take my hand, and I will
guide you to paradise. I will walk and talk to you each and
every day and know that I will behold your face, and being in
your presence is what I long for. I will bow to you and sing a
joyful song, and yes I know that it will be a brighter day. To
know that I will get to live a brand-new life in a wonderful
place from hurt, harm, and danger will be the best place to
place my feet. To live free from sin where no one can take
you, where you dare not want to go a place for you and a place
just for me. A brighter day is where I know He will take care
and cover me. Brighter day is what I want to see, and I know
it will be all I can imagine—a place for me as well as a place
for you. Trust in him, and you will see that day real soon.

To be Kept by Jesus

I am a woman. A strong woman. A woman of God who was kept by Jesus. I am a woman. A strong woman. Not black, white, or even Hispanic but a true woman of God. I am a woman who stands tall now and on a firm foundation. I will stand strong, tall, and proud no matter what man has done to me. As long as I shall live, I will cleave to you, Lord, and hasten to your every throne. No matter how tired or even sick I should get, I will cleave to thee, Lord. Lord, I know you have pity and heard my cry and have protected me thus this far from all the dangers that seem to come my way. I put my trust in a man, and it seemed like that man let me down every time. Thinking that I could find true love from them, but it was not so. You were all the love I needed to help to see me through all I was going through. I do know now that if I just give you the opportunity to do just what you said you would and grab onto your hand, you will guide me and lead me through whatever deep, dark valley or high mountains or even tortuous alleys are there. Unknowing what lies ahead, I will ask the Lord Almighty to keep me strong and keep me covered with his grace and his mercy.

Lord, you know my weakness and all my doubts that I have stored in me, but through all of that please help me, pick me up, shake me off, and put me back on the right track. You know what is in my future, which I myself have not the knowledge but will trust and depend on you, and no longer man who has let me down every time. I am truly covered by your blood and have no more fears, no more pain, and hurt that had me feeling like I could not go on any further. Oh, but I truly *made it, and my soul said yes. Yes to your will, to all of your ways, you, Lord, have covered me and brought me out of all danger and harm that I truly went through, and I truly am grateful to you, Lord. So whatever your will is for me, I will get ready for a long journey that lies before me. I will continue to open my mouth and give you all the praises because you did not have to do it, but you did. It was your amazing grace that brought me where I am now—strong, proud, and tall and only depending on you to help me make it through.*

God said he will fight all my battles if I just let him, and now I will, Lord, because to be kept by Jesus is an awesome thing. To have my mind, peace, love, and joy, Lord, you will give it all to me and more. So hide me in your safety in a secret place from harm, Because you have totally covered me when I lost my mind, when I should have been killed, when I went through what mind did to me and even the sickness I went through, you covered me. When I even felt all alone and felt no one knew what I was feeling, you were there and yes you keep me, Lord. So let the Lord fight for you, and you sit back and take the ride.

Nobody but God

Nobody **but** God did it, and I truly can see it. God has brought me through it all, and I am still standing and a living testimony for you to see he did it for me and yes, he can do the same for you. Those who knew me and knew me well can surely tell you the pain, struggles, and all of the experiences that I went through. Thinking that a man could make me feel complete was not quite the answer and did not give me closure in my life. I thought that to have a man was a great thing, and as many women would say take what you get and move on. I thought as some of us women do: if you tell the truth and not sugar coat it, you would say that if you just have a piece of a man, you have something that others try to have. Not true, oh so not true.

Some men will take you to a level that you have and probably would not ever get to complete, and some will take you to a level where they themselves will truly complete. The levels may be too high for you to cross over and to go through, so you have to learn to keep your mind stayed basically on depending and fighting for yourself. Find the master, is what I would hear, and when you find him, get deep and he will be near. Don't give up and don't give in, and please make sure you don't let that man win. So I stood back and threw my hands up and put my focus on God, and right then I knew I had to make that serious call.

Nobody **but** God took me, washed me up, and cleaned me

up and told me oh how sweet I could be with just having him in my life and beside me. The only man in my life that I needed then and from this day forth was the Lord himself because as we know an earthly man will do you wrong, leave you, and put you out to dry. An earthly man will do to you what the father in heaven would not dare to dream of. Earthly men will hide; cheat, steal, kill, and yes destroy your entire life if you are not strong enough to stop him before he has taken you to the point of no return.

See, what I thought I was missing in a man was there all the time. No matter how low down I thought I had gotten and how ugly my face would be sometimes when the tears would flow down, there was a man waiting for me to call. I searched and searched, going from man to man, seeking something that I thought I could truly find.

I did not understand that if I stopped, sat down, and prayed, the Lord would hear all my cries. So one day while I was sitting in my lonely room dark and full of fear, I decided to fall on my knees. I said, "Father if you could so ever hear me, then hear me now as I call. I am your child who has been seeking comfort, peace, and love that only you can give. Please, when you pass down this lonely street, just stop and make one last house call. If you should knock, I will let you in. I know only you can save me, clean me up, and make me whole again. Nobody **but** you is all I need."

Nobody **but** you, Lord, it was nobody **but** you, because after the coma I learned that when you came, you gave me another chance in life. Until you send me a man to love, I promise not to go back to a place full of darkness and hatred. But God, the one after the coma the almighty one who took what I did before that coma and now forgave me of it all. Let no man take you down the dusty, long, dreary road again; let him not be able to beat and tell you that you will never be anything without him. God is all you need to get through the day, months, and years to come, and hold on so you can see the sun. God will turn your long midnights into days, when it seems all hope is lost and can't find your way. Nobody did it, **but** God and nobody else will. I call, and I know he is always there to catch me when I fall. So lean on me, I heard him say; talk to me each and every day. Let me walk with you, and you can hold my hand, and I in my word will help you to stand. **But** God who now has changed this bitter, scorned woman frown into a smile, for nobody **but** God is my total life. For you, Lord, I will live, and for you, Lord, I truly will die. Nobody **but** God has my fight.

What Kinda Journey

It's a long day's journey, but I will be oh so fine.
It's a long day's journey, I will be just fine.
It's a rough road to hike, but with the keeper,
the Lord, on my side, I will make it in time,
and I promise not to get left behind.
It's a long day's journey, and yes I will be oh so fine.
I know that my mother will be waiting, and my father
as well, so I want to be ready to go on that great journey
one day, and it just might be soon and right on time.
I can hear my sister and my brother calling on me,
saying, "Come on, and let's go see our King, the
one who died, hung his head high, bled for me,
and the same one who died and bled for you."
There is a journey I want to take, and when I get there,
I want to see those streets that I heard were paved with
gold. The sun will be shining, and I am not talking
about the sun, I am talking about the Son who is filled
with glory, shining like a morning star from afar.
I look forward to taking that journey that was
set only for me, and the one that was set just
for you will be your personal journey too.
At the end of the road, the journey that we will have
to take will come to a halt where we will stop and hear

his voice, and his voice so mighty and so sweet will say, "Your journey is complete, so now you must rest." Rest on this side to never see any more, but to cross over to a great place where there is joy, love, and tranquility. For as I say to you and also to me, let your day's journey be filled with the things of God's will and not yours; live for his purpose and his purpose alone, and ask for that strength that only the Lord can give.

When you cross the end of the road to study war no more, lay down your shield and turn it in so you can walk on the streets that are paved with pure gold. Happiness, joy, love, and peace in that place where you will be, with the master is who I really want to see. To see my father is what I long for, so I will keep on this journey.

Though it may get rough sometimes, I will hold on. Now I lay me down to sleep, and I will try not to weep, for the Father will wipe every tear from my eyes and reward me in the sky with a wonderful prize that will only be for me and me alone. Just to be with him is the best prize I could receive, and just to hear his voice say, "Well done, well done, my good and faithful servant, come on in, come on in. Come on in from this journey that may have taken you through the toils of life and all of your heartache and pain. Come on in from the journey. Pace yourself and sit, my child, next to me and my Father who has resided on the throne. Come on in and wipe your feet and take a seat, and let's sing joyful songs of sweet praise." So one day you will have to say to your family, "My journey is now ended, and I must tell you all goodbye, and please get your house in order so that when you complete your journey you can see me at home. Goodbye, family, I will always love you, but yes my work down here is complete and I am gone. Gone to be with my father, who sits high on the throne." No more will I have to endure, and no more suffering will I have to take, for my Master said you have finished this journey so let's come on and go home. A place of peace and rest is where I must go, and I know I want to hear him say, "Well done, come on in from your long journey and be with me forever more."

Still Here

Although I have been through all that was placed in front of me, I'm still here by God's grace and his mercy. Though the mountains seemed so hard to climb, even when I tied the rope around my waist and threw the other end to latch on to the top, it felt like with each climb I was sliding down more and more and unable to reach what was in front of me. It seemed as though when I reached a puddle in front of me, it turned into a great river, and no matter the size of my boat and how many floaters I had on, it felt like I was drowning, going deeper and deeper to the bottom. Even though I had a car and it helped me to get around so easy, I felt like I was using my feet like the Flintstones, and it took days to reach my destination.

I woke one night and heard a sweet voice come to me and say, "Trust in me, and you will never feel the same again. Lean on me and hold on to me tight and don't let go." As I took that and pondered it in my heart and heard and trusted in Jesus, my days were filled with so much joy and happiness. I'm still here to do a work for my father, and I will fight until my victory is won and my destiny is complete. I am still here by his grace and by his mercy, and it has taken me this far. Still I am able to wake up and place my feet on the ground with open eyes and a voice to speak and say, "Father, it's in your name that I can still be able to run the race that is presented before me. I still am here to go out and do your will and seek after my brothers and sisters and let

them know that if they just seek you, they will truly find just what they need. Despite what the enemy thought he could do to me, I am still in battle for you, and you are my protector like you were with David and Goliath." So I say
I am here by his Grace
I am here by his Mercy
The love that you have shown me helped me to endure this race through sunshine or rain. Through all my trails, I made it through. I even struggled through all my illnesses. When the doctors said no, you said yes to see me through. As I struggled through being put out at night to have harm easily come to me, you covered me and protected me from all the danger that lurked around about me. Though friends and family set me to the side and walked away, you have been there with me the entire time. I'll still love you in spite of all the pain, and though my situation was not for me to handle and I wanted to throw in the towel, I heard you call out to me and say my name so loud. You said, "Tonya, my child, hold on and don't give up. Ride this race, take a seat to the side, and let me guide you all the way. Don't let go, just hold on, and I will see you through." Weeping may endure for a night, and it didn't say how long the night would be. But joy when it comes will come in the morning.
Rejoice because the problem was not bigger
than God, and that is why I'm still here.
Here to speak the word
Here to give the Love
Here to help others
Here to fight on, not give in nor give up.
I will not let go **BUT** I will let
God
Here for my brother and my sister too
Here for you and know that I am living
Because of you
I heard the voice say it to me, and that is
why I'm still here for you and for me.

Scorned Woman

When you think that you have a great man, it hurts when it doesn't turn out in the best interest for your life. Not giving it to God and allowing Him to be the head and in control will take you to places that you should not go. I remember meeting my husband in the apartment that I had recently moved in with my babies. If I had just waited for the man that God would have sent to me, it would have turned out for the best. Not finding out the real person that this man was took me down another rough road.

Healing is what was needed for me, and I did not do that. To take time out and let everything mend to where it needed to be is what I should have done. Mending my mind to where I could think clear thoughts again is what was needed of me, and oh how crazy I was to let myself go through another rollercoaster cycle.

I met this man when he came to my door in 1992 to retrieve a pair of hair clippers that I had recently borrowed from his aunt. I just wanted to feel like I was loved and wanted, not rejected and alone. You know, as women we never want to be alone, no matter how much we tell others "I don't need a man because I can do it all on my own." No matter how I look at it, I did not want to be by myself, so I went through another relationship without stepping back and taking a peek at what this man had to offer, not just for myself, but my babies as well.

So I let him in and started dating him and doing things to make me feel happy. The sexual needs are what I was starting to only care about, so I pushed my feelings to the backburner and didn't care anymore how this man would treat me. I wanted this, and I did not care; I just wanted to be loved and nothing else from him, so I closed out the emotional part of me and only opened up the sexual part that I knew could not be hurt.

Now, this man could do all the things in bed to a woman, but that is not all that I needed. When I look back, I realize that I was not looking at the signs that were approaching. I can't say that I was stupid; I just wanted to be loved, and that is what I thought was going on at that particular time.

If I had looked at the first sign, I could have saved myself from the hurt that would come later. He started staying out all night drinking and then I found out he smoked cigarettes and weed. I chose to stay and deal with it because he was there, and I did not want to be the one without a man.

The clouds in my life started getting dark, and now the tears were about to start flowing. I should have let Jesus be my guide. I know that if I would have given all my problems and troubles to the Lord, he would have guided me out quickly and safely. My God can see way down the road, but I stopped going to church and believing that all would be well if I just let it.

This man ended up in jail for approximately fifteen months, and at that time I should have left him, but I still stuck in there because I had invested some years into this relationship and I wanted to try to make it work. I went to the jail every week to see him and accepted the calls and the letters because all he had was me. No one else stood by him, and I knew how it felt to be alone. After he was released, he asked me to marry him, and I said yes. He got a job, and I had one, and we tried to do all we could to make ends meet. With the help of my aunt, I put a small wedding together, and my sister was there also to stand next to me, and that was a joyful but sad occasion to me. I do love my sister and that meant the world to me that she was next to me by my side, but my mother was not. She told me that if I didn't marry him, she would do certain things to help me. But she hadn't been there for me before, so I knew she wouldn't be there for me then or later. My dad showed up late, so my boys gave me away.

This man would eventually go on to messing around with different women. He started working at Grandy's restaurant on Seminary Drive in Fort Worth, Texas and boy he thought I was a fool. We moved in Everman, Texas and, of course, there were women who stayed down from us that he got acquainted with. I found out through a phone call that he was cheating on me, and while I was at work he would take the car, and have the children sometimes, and go to another woman's house.

I found this woman's address, and I went over to her place. We had a few words, and I told her to call him on his house phone right then, and I would be on the other end when he answered. He picked up and answered, and he started talking nice and sweet to her, and I busted him, and he hung up. I went home and packed all his belongings into trash bags and placed them in the trunk of the car, and took them to his job at Grandys resturant and threw them in front of the door and told him to go live with her, and I left. Crying tears and barely being able to drive, I finally made it home. My heart felt like it was being ripped out and torn into pieces. I felt betrayed and wondered why did he do this to me? What did I do to deserve this? As I lay through the night, he would repeatedly call me saying, "I am sorry, sorry for what I did. Can I come home? I won't do it again."

Being the fool that I was, I took him back and thought that I could change this man and make it work because we were married, and I didn't want to get a divorce. I wanted my marriage to work. As we know, if it is not of God, it will not work. God has to be the control, the head, the entire center, the beginning and the end.

My mother died in 1998 at the age of forty-eight in a motor vehicle accident in Fort Worth around the Sun Valley area where a bus driver from Fort Worth ISD was involved, as she was leaving a modeling studio where she help run it with her boyfriend at the time. It was around the Easter week approaching that was the hardest time of my life. I was going through all the heartaches and the torture, both physically and mentally. I was not close to my mom even though I tried my hardest to receive the love I found myself as I got older given more of me and not really receiving anything back in return. I would always be there for her regardless of how I felt that was my mom and I loved her dearly. She would call me in the middle of the night and I knew that this was only when she was unable to get my sister or my sister could not come , and I would go and see when would my mom tell me when she called me to do something for her. There were times I would have to go to her house and when I got there one particular time my mom needed her tire changed and that man that was residing with her at the time was sitting at the table doing some paper work and he would not get up to help her. Wow I said mom I have to bring my husband over and we did not mind changing your tire and that man is in the house and don't wont to help you that is not right. You don't even like my husband but he is here for you, you didn't come to my wedding but he is here for you as usual. I confronted the man in the house and told him she is and will always be my mother and you will not hurt her she is too good to you for you to do what you are doing to her and I will fight you over my mother. As you all know I was put out of the house but that was my mother and like she felt towards me I did not want to see her hurt.

When my husband and I separated, I moved in with my dad who was a bitter man, and was verbally and physically abusive to me and the children, but I had no other option at the time. While I was with my dad, my husband ended up getting into trouble again, and I visited him in jail, but I was lonely. I met a young man, and he was nice to me, and I had a small affair. I meet this man at the car wash on East Berry in Fort Worth where everyone at that time would hang out on the weekends. This man was three years younger than I and to me at that time did not mean anything especially when I felt the way I did feeling not loved and lots of pain and hurt from the one man I was married to but left. I eventually broke it off with him after only two months only using him for a sex toy when I needed a fix and wanted to be satisfied and nothing more, and any way when I left my husband he went to jail for unknown reason that I did not know about but he did not stay in too long for me a couple of months sitting in a cell being taking care of and no worries about what you have done or the chaos you create not long enough to sit there no isolation and no meditation on life and the real meaning of life. I told my husband, and he forgave me which at that time I felt he should have after all the things he put me through. After he got out of jail, we moved into my mom's house right after the funeral; I am glad I got away from my dad, because he was verbally and physically abusive while we were there with him. I recall one night he went into the kid's room late night and woke up my oldest son and tried to get him to try on some clothes he had, but it was late, and my son said he would try on the clothes in the morning. My dad started hitting my son and put him in a neck hold, waking up the entire house because of the screaming. My younger son went to help his brother and ended up picking my dad up and slamming him to the floor to try and get his brother loose from my father choking him. We all ran outside, and the police came and arrested my dad for violence.

So this is when I ended up moving into my mom's house and my husband came with us. I got pregnant again, and we were both excited, or so I thought. Then one night, I received a phone call. The person said, "Do you know what your husband is doing?" I said, "No, who is this?" But they hung up. Then another night, I received another phone call, and it was the same voice and the same person stating, "Do you know what your husband is doing? He is doing it with me." I confronted my husband, but he denied it. Then I received another call, and that time she gave me her name and said she was pregnant with his baby. I went to his job, because this female worked with him and I needed to do this in person with the both of them. I asked him, and he said no. We argued for a bit, but then I left and went home. When he came home, he told me, "You will not mess up what I have. You make me sick, and I will do whatever I want to you." Then he pushed me; I fought back, and he punched me in the stomach, which caused me to have some pain and discomfort. I had to call the doctor, and I ended up being rushed to the hospital. I was losing the baby and bleeding tremendously. I had to stay in the hospital because I would not stop bleeding and I ended up having a miscarriage losing the baby we both once wanted together.

I started wondering whether I should give up and let go, or fight and hold on to my marriage. I was confused and alone with no help. My mind was wondering, and now my sister wanted to sell the house we are in. Knowing that I and my family had nowhere to go and I had been putting a lot of money into moms house to keep it fixed up and it did need some repairs from roofing to plumbing. My sister felt that she would not be able to come over and I said to myself you don't see me anyway and you have a place and mom is no longer here just let me stay, and I can buy you out if needed. No, the ideas did not work so I went and consulted an attorney to try and keep the house in the family and I was willing to make sure my husbands name would not be on any legal documents only my sisters name would appear on the paperwork if something should happen to me. I knew that my mom worked hard on keeping the house for my sister and me if we would ever need a place to stay so I thought, my thoughts are always outweighed. So the house was sold, and my family and I moved to a townhome on the West side of Fort Worth off of Vickery Blvd.

Just when I thought it could not get any worse, he did it again—more women, more dugs, and more fun for him. He lost his job, and I was the bread winner again. I got tired of the late nights and decided what I should do. His aunt came by one day and invited me to go to prayer and church with her. I said, "Yes I will go. Will it hurt?" I was tired with my life, and it seemed as though my life was not going anywhere, and I needed some help. I needed Jesus, and I found Him.

Now, He never left me; I left Him, thinking that I could handle it all on my own. I was crying all night long and did not know who to turn to, where to go, or what to do. I went to prayer, and I received the Holy Ghost that day because I went there for a purpose, and it was to seek Jesus for him to fix me and take control of my life. I said, "I need to walk close to you, God, and at this particular time, nothing else matters." As I entered the church I went looking for something. As I knelt down on the altar, I felt as though someone was standing beside me, and a warm touch came all over me, and I was trying to shake it off. I heard Him say, "If you follow me, I will lead you in the right way, and you will never have to be lonely again. But you have to believe that I can and will do all things only if you believe in your heart I am who I say I am. I will give you the desires of your heart. Trust me, my child, the things that you went through was just for a season. Let me help bring you to a place of peace and love."

As I was on my knees, I could feel something different, and it felt like my burdens were being lifted away from me. Tears were flowing, but I felt unspeakable joy on the inside. I just wanted to get up and run. My hands were clapping, my tongue spoke of another language, but I understood what it was saying deep down in my heart, "Follow me, hear me, and I will guide you in the right path." I understood what was being said, and I took Him at his word this time, not wanting to turn around no matter how hard, how painful, how many tears I may have to cry but knowing the comfort of His love and the mercy and the grace that He will give to me each and every day. "That is what I will long for with you, Father. I am ready to do your will, obey, and abide." So I did, but it wasn't easy.

I remember reading my Bible and going to church, but still dealing with the issues at home. I remember learning a particular scripture in the Bible and keeping it in my head and saying it when I felt down and out. This song that came in my mind when my heart felt heavy and broken and I kept the scripture near and dear in my mind and heart.

> I am going to wait on the Lord
> I am going to wait on the Lord until I die
> Oh, I am going to wait on the Lord
> I will wait on the Lord until I die
> I am going to see His face
> I am going to see His face
> I am going to see his face one day, oh yes
> I am going wait, fight, and pray until I die

> Book of Isaiah 40: 28-31
> Hast thou not known? Hast thou not heard,
> That the everlasting God, the Lord, the Creator of the
> ends of the earth fainteth not neither is weary?
> There is no searching of his understanding
> He giveth power to the faint; and to them that
> have no might he increaseth strength.
> Even the youths shall faint and be weary
> and the young men shall utterly fall;
> But they that wait upon the Lord shall renew their strength;
> They shall mount up with wings as eagles;
> they shall run, and not be weary; and
> They shall walk, and not faint.

I began to go to church all the time, whenever the church doors were open and I did not have to work. I often sang, especially when I am down and out.

Singing was what helped me, and it felt like I could get what I needed from a song and that the Lord was talking to me through a certain lyric. Oh, how I loved it when my children and grandbabies were small. I would hold them and sing to them all the time; that was our bonding time together. I remember going to six flags and opening up for Kirk Franklin before he came on stage, and that was an honor for me. I would go to the churches and sing, and they would have a mass choir that was made up of different people from different churches, and I was there also. Now, I just came back from backsliding out of the church and still need that push to stay with the Lord, so I went to church every chance I got.

I still was singing with the choir, and upon going through what I had at home I found myself just trying to stay close to church, but I was very lonely. I did something that I thought I would never do to my husband: I committed adultery. He was a man who was kind, sweet, and handsome. I was only looking for friendship, but it turned out to be something more than that. That friendship grew to be a six-month affair, and I felt good at the time and only cared about my own desires. I always said a woman could do the same as a man, but better and never get caught unless she lets her guard down. This man moved to Oklahoma, and I kept in touch with him through it all. Every Saturday I drove from Fort Worth to Oklahoma City to meet up with him. I was living two worlds and handling it quite well. I no longer wanted to be with my husband, and it wasn't so much because of the new man, but because I realized that I could actually be happy. Whenever I was leaving to go back home, I felt guilty, and it was eating me up inside. I knew it was wrong and that God was not pleased with me. What do you do when you find yourself somewhere you don't need to be, but like it where you are and nothing can change your mind? I started sliding away from church. I found out that I was pregnant in the year that I was having the affair in the year of 2003 and unsure who the father was and did not care because I knew I was not going to carry the fetus and I was a couple of weeks because I was late and took a test I felt something will happen I just knew it always does that the way I felt about my life at that moment.

I made my mind up to tell my husband that I no longer want to be with this other man. I didn't want to be the one to destroy it, not when I fought to keep it together. So I told the guy in Oklahoma that I no longer wanted to continue our affair and would not be able to see him again. He was not happy. I drove up to Oklahoma one more time to be with him and to tell him I was pregnant and that I must make my marriage work. He agreed, and I went back home to tell my husband what was taking place. I went home thinking of how to approach him and tell him about the affair and the pregnancy. He came home late that night, and I was already asleep. When he came upstairs to the room, he was high and smelling of alcohol, and I said to myself, "No, he is back to his old ways. It was just a phase he was going through, and I tried, but I need to tell him to leave." As he lay down, I arose and said, "I no longer want to be married. You will have to leave and, oh, by the way, I am pregnant, and you will not and cannot stay here."

He jumped up and said, "What, girl, what is your problem?"

I said, "I'm tired. I don't want you. I have being seeing someone, and you will have to go." He got up and started after me and pushing on me, and I had to fight him off.

He went outside and started banging on cars, hitting the walls of the house, and cursing and screaming.

I called the police and got a report, and I called my friend and told him what occurred. He said, "You will have to move because you won't get any peace."

So I stayed with friends and got some of my things while he was gone one day. My friend came from Oklahoma to help me move and to stay with me for a couple of days to make sure I was okay, and my boys were back and forward from their best friend and my father's house, as my baby girl was living with me but would go to my dad's house time to time because the kids still attended school in the Southwest side of town as they were in Middle and High School. When I went through the house, I saw that my husband had bleached the furniture and my clothes that were still there. He ripped the mattress and damaged a lot of things in the apartment. As we were going up the stairs, there were piles of cigarettes and a chair by the window as though he was waiting on me to come home.

I thought I was about to start a new phase in my life by leaving my husband for good. But it didn't turn out as I expected because I was not going to church like I should have, and I was married and having an affair,, finding myself still in love with my husband and pregnant. . At first I was okay, but I became very sick and was missing work, and not feeling myself. I was to be judged by God.

Colossians 4:25 KJV
But he that doeth wrong shall receive for the wrong which he hath done; and there is no respect of persons
Colossians 2:21 KJV
Touch not; taste not; handle not
Colossians 2:23 KJV
Which things have indeed a shew of wisdom in will-worship, and humility, and neglecting of the body; not in any honour to the satisfying of the flesh

All in doing wrong and leaving the church, God had to show me again what He could do and is in charge of. I remember getting really sick, and I don't recall much, but my daughter and my sons had to help me. I do remember driving and not feeling myself. I had lost the baby prior to this due to complications unknown I just miscarried and was only less than eight weeks along , and I felt as though my life was going nowhere, and I wanted to give it all up. See, when you take yourself out of the will of God, things tend to happen beyond your control. All I remember is driving and crying, and I still don't recall anything beyond this point other than what was told to me by my husband and children.

My husband yes the one man I was still married to and the man that I did not want any more came back the man I had the affair on moved to the new apartment, and they said that I had lost my mind; I could not even take care of myself, and I was not to be alone. So he came back to help the children with me so that my daughter could go to school and the boys would not have to do it on their own. They said he took care of me. I cannot recall any of this. I was told he was sad and he took me to the church and they prayed for me. I do know that if you don't do right by God, he brings you to your lowest, and you will raise your eyes up and ask Him to help you. No other help can you get anywhere else but from Him.

James 5:14-15 KJV
Is any sick among you? Let him call for the elders of the church; and let them pray over him, anointing him with oil in the name of the Lord. And the prayer of faith shall save the sick, and the Lord shall raise him up; and if he have committed sins, they shall be forgiven.

I got my memory back, but I do not know how or what took place prior to that. All I know is that I am thankful that God brought me back.

Psalms 1:14 1:4-5 KJV
Blessed is the man that walketh not in the counsel of the ungodly, not standeth in the way of sinners, nor sitteth in the seat of the scornful.
Hear me when I call, O God of my righteousness; thou hast enlarged me when I was in distress; have mercy upon me, and hear my prayer.
Give ear to my words, O Lord, consider my meditation.

My husband and I ended up back together once again, because I told myself that he really cared for me. But soon enough, it was back to the old games. Same old, same old, is where he took me back, but I never went back to doing what I used to do. I wanted to serve God until I died, and

I meant that with all my heart. We moved again and again, and the old life with my husband was back—the staying out late, the friends, and family coming by all the time and never spending the quality time with me. Nothing mattered to him, but he just kept saying, "I can have whom I want and I can do what I want, and you will accept it and shut up." The name calling began, and the hits also, and it made me feel as though I was living in the past.

It's All About You

I wanted to better myself, and I started going to school and working part time, and my husband was working driving trucks. While in school in the year of 2005 at the age of 37 years old I was about to start doing Externship for a Certified Medical Assistant and loving what I do which was helping people, and about to graduate, finding out that we were about to have our first grandbaby due May of 2006 from my oldest son. My son had already graduated and was great in school; he and my other children did not give me any problems at all. He was a saxophone player, and my other sons played the trumpet. I graduated from Medical Assistance School attending Remington College in Fort Worth with a 4.0.

Now while enjoying my new career first volunteering 2005 then I was hired to start working 2006 in January at JPS and my first grandson was born February of 2006 proud grandmother of a big bouncing baby boy. My baby girl who was sixteen years of age who was still in high school was pregnant around the same time as my oldest son girlfriend had a bouncing baby boy born in November 2006, and I was very happy and excited not about the age of her being a mother while young but we have a little baby 24- seven in the house, maybe this baby will bring life and joy to us all, especially my husband having a grandson in the house just maybe he will straighten up for the baby's sake. My husband began stealing from me and making me think that I was going crazy. My son had a saxophone that the school had given him to play, and it came up missing. My movies and money and other items started to come up missing as time went on; by then, I really knew it was him No one had broken into the house that we were staying in located in Forest Hill, Texas as I was on housing but paying eighty percent of the rent, I did a police report, and he was angry saying, "Why are you doing a report? Maybe your son has it." We finally moved out of the house because I felt that why am I paying the majority of the rent I may as well find somewhere else and the landlord never wanted to fix the things that were given us problems in the house, so yes here we go again looking for a home that we can try to settle down in and be at peace. He never admitted it, though. We moved into a house that I was trying to rent to own and it was very nice located in Everman, Texas. The rent was $1,200 dollars a month, and that was a lot, but we could manage it together, so I thought. This man was working at Ben E. Keith driving and making good money, but he lost his job because he was trying to steal. He was a driver and delivery man, and he was given a check from a vendor to pay for the pickup. He put the check in his pocket and went about the following pickups. When he finished his routes and the day ended, he came home, pulled the check-out of his pocket, and laid it on the dresser. I noticed it and told him take it back right away, and let them know he forgot he had it in his pocket.

As the days went by, I thought he had turned the check in, but he hadn't. They called him to the office and he was fired. Now, once again, I was the breadwinner with expensive rent and bills, a daughter, and a grandson my daughter's baby all under one roof, along with a man who put himself in this predicament and did nothing about it. Having fun and staying at home is what it was all about for him; it looked as though he had given up and liked staying home and having me take care of him, but that got old very soon.

I decided to give it all up and move to where I could afford it. We moved into a duplex, and from there it got worse and worse. Now this time it was not just him, but the daughter too. I was so into church, and praying is what I did and had to do because I was giving up on my marriage. How can you when the other doesn't want to? I was tired of the abuse, the struggles, the ridiculing, and the torment. The good book says in Colossians 3:19-20:

Husbands, love your wives and be not bitter against them Children, obey your parents in all things; for this is well pleasing unto the Lord

So not with just the husband, but I was having to fight a battle with my daughter. I saw that she was looking for love from a man as well, and I stuck by her side in the midst of all the things we went through together as mother and daughter. I felt I needed to stick with her, because I knew she would need me. My daughter looked into getting her own place and she was seventeen at the time because she felt it was time. She wanted to be on her own so she found a place in Fort Worth off of Mansfield Hwy and Miller Street where they went based on your income, and all I did was filled out a portion of the form. She applied for an apartment and government assistance and did receive all needed to help her along with my assistance when needed. I helped my daughter move into her first apartment with no other assistance and had to be at work the following morning and yes I was tired but it was all for her and the baby.

Finally I moved out but not having a place to go because I had left my husband again because of the drugs and the lies. I moved out of the duplex where my husband and I were staying to try to see if I can do better with my life because I felt I was going down and he was the cause of it all, but I had nowhere to go. I went to stay with my daughter, and I had to pray and ask God to help me and give me my own so that I may be comfortable. In the midst of it all, my oldest son got married, and I moved alone into a very nice community where I could call my own and I was ready to start a new life. Separated from my husband and beginning a new chapter in my life was exciting to me for the first time—no other man involved- and I was trying to pick up the pieces in my life and take it day by day with the help of God. I would speak with my husband on the phone, but it was only for a short time.

In an instant, when it seemed like all was going well, I ended up getting sick and going to the doctor and having an emergency surgery that would keep me off work for several weeks and in need of assistance around the house. My husband came over and took me to the hospital, and my children were there, as well as my father. My husband did not have a car, so he had to drive my van to take me to the hospital. I remember going in being scared and not knowing what the outcome was going to be, but I was a praying woman, and I learned how to call on the name of Jesus when I needed Him.

I made it out to find out by my children that my husband had left with my van. What a feeling! It hurt worse than the knife that cut me from one end of my stomach to the other. I prayed in my room when night fell and said, "I have been here, Lord, and have done all that you tell me to do. Now be with me as I go through this journey. I will not be alone because you are here with me now. Guide me, hold me, and pick me if I should fall. Wipe my tears and lead me on my way. Shine in me, Lord, that when people see me they won't see sickness, they won't see man, and they will see you, Jesus, the Jesus that lives in me. I will bless you, oh my Father up in heaven."

> I've been through the storm and rain
> I made it
> You ask me how, in Jesus's name
> I made it
> I've had so many ups and so many downs, and I was leveled to the ground, but through it

all
I made it
My loved ones walked out on me
I made it
God gave me the victory
I made it
I have had so many ups and so many downs
But thank you, Jesus, through it all
I made it

I was taken home by my baby son and daughter. My dad stepped in when I needed him without me even asking, and he covered my bills and food expenses. This was a tremendous blessing. While I was down, I would, and even still, say these words:

Psalms 23: 1-6
The Lord is my shepherd; I shall not want,
He maketh me to lie down in green pastures;
he leadeth me beside the still waters,
He restoreth my soul; he leadeth me in the
paths of righteousness for his name's sake.
Yea, though I walk through the valley of the shadow of death,
I will fear no evil for thou art with me; thy
rod and thy staff they comfort me,
Thou preparest a table before me in the presence of mine
enemies; thou anointest my head with oil my cup runneth over
Surley goodness and mercy shall follow me all the days of
my life; and I will dwell in the house of the Lord forever.

I know that God will cover me under the blood and I will be safe in His arms. No matter what I go through and how I feel, He is my Shepherd, and I have all that I need in Him. He restores my failing health and gives me peace, and I am safe in His arms. When the storms seem like they are raging, and I feel that the enemy came to try to destroy me, no weapon formed against me shall prosper. I will have eternal life with you. Until then, hide me in your bosom and keep me safe. I will give you all the glory, and all the honor goes to you. Worthy is the name of the Lord, and there is no one else like you. All I need is you, Lord, in my life. Help me, Father, I cry out to thee.

Now, Father, I need you to help him and come in right now and comfort, because no one else likes you and there is nothing you cannot do. We need you to come in right now was my words. My son has been there for me when I needed him even thought I will find out something that will take me to another level in my life. I am here for you son momma is here, now help us God through this. It seems like when you have been through one, you have to go through another, but all the test and trial help you to get stronger. God will never put more on you than you can bear.

All your help comes from God, and I am so glad that He is there for me and knowing that He has picked me up and turned me around and has placed my feet on a solid ground, and I will never worry about what will go in my life ahead.

I moved to another apartment, which ended up being in the same complex as my son who would move in his own place after living with me for a moment. Yet I often felt so lonely and discouraged. I kept telling myself that Jesus, The Comforter, is all that I needed, and I could go to him when in need.

I found out that my husband was back in town. At this point I had been doing so well; there was no man in my life, and I was closest to God.

Now, let me show you what happened: I know I am a child of God no matter what someone has done to me. In spite of it all, I have God in my heart and in my life. My husband fell ill, and we found out that he needed to have a pacemaker implanted. So I took him back, feeling that still being his wife, it was what I should do. I went to the hospital with him and stayed with him through his surgery. I heard God say, *No matter what happened, I am about to make you better, my child. I've got you, and, no matter what the condition may look like, it is well.*

So he went into surgery and made it out, and I took my husband home where I had move into an apartment on the far west side of Fort Worth near the Las Vegas Trail. I fed, washed, and took care of him. . He had some ups and downs with the device, and I watched him cry some nights, but I stuck by his side no matter what the cost. I wondered if he felt guilty about how he did me; I don't even think it crossed his mind. As time progressed, he began to get better. I figured there'd be no more alcohol, no more smoking; it was all going to be better. My oldest son at this time was on hard times and had custody of his two children and needed a place for a moment to stay for the three of them. My husband was not working so as my son went to work in the am and I went to work also my husband would watch the babies till one of us would get off and come back to the house to relieve him of his duties as a grandfather. The effect my son had on me and his two children living with him was hard to deal with, because we never knew what he was going to do. I learned feeling no love and losing someone who means a lot to you will lead you to do things that may not be of you, and you may take avenues that make you feel like you have taken a trip to space but everyone goes through losing a spouse from separation you must get passed it and move on I told my son. But then my husband changed quickly and started going back into the old person that he was. He found new friends that were not so good, and it seemed like they were doing worse, and it rubbed off on him. But I realized it was already there. It was just surfacing again to let me know it never left.

My son was involved in my life a great deal because he had custody of his children, and he needed a baby sitter as he went to work. So my husband ended up watching the children for him since he was not working after his procedure. At this particular time, the family received two bouncing baby boys after the loss of the two we had to bury: one from my baby boy in 2006 and the other from my youngest daughter. We were elated with the new birth of the twins, and that made it a little better while going through the joy and pain of life.

So I helped our son watch the babies, but on the days he did not have anything to do nor work I thought that he was finding a job so that he could help around the house, he was up to his old tricks again. When I found out, I was tired and said regardless of my son needing help, we would work this one out. So I fell down on my knees and asked the Father up above to help me. I need your amazing grace. I need some help. I had to morn a lot of time so that the devil would not come in and try to destroy me. I needed my Father, and He is about to do it. I prayed and fasted, prayed and fasted, and said whatever your will is let it be done and not mine but your will Lord. Please, Jesus, remove all that is not like you. Remove it out of my heart, mouth, mind, body, and especially my home. Please, Sir Jesus, remove it right now in the name of the Father, Son, and the Holy Ghost. I am fed up with all that I am going through, and I need you. Little did I know, God had already begun to work it out.

So one day my husband picked me up from work and was late as usual. I could feel that there was something wrong. I could not put my finger on it, but it was heavy in the house. I felt it when I walked around, and I could sense that something was about to happen. This man would walk me into a darkness filled with hate and almost death. We were having a little dispute, and I sat down and told him that he needed to leave, and I no longer wanted to be with him, because he was not going to do right by me and that it was finally over.

I told him that we could remain friends, but he did not want to hear what I was saying. Before I knew it, I was sitting in the chair in the living area next to the play pen, and he jumped on me and began choking me, and he was choking so hard that it felt like I was leaving my body. I could not breathe, and I remember saying, "Stop! You are hurting me! Stop! Get off of me. You are hurting me!" My grandson was sleeping, and I was trying to get up and away to make sure he would be okay. He was saying, "If I can't have you, no one will. I will kill you, girl, I will kill you." He said this in a voice that did not belong to him anymore, a voice that sounded like something from a horror movie. As he's chocking me his grip was getting harder and harder as my body was hanging over the chair and the top part of me was in between the playpen and the side of the chair. I was speaking to God, "Please help me. He is trying to kill me. I have let go, and I let you now work this situation out for me. I don't want to leave. Help me. I don't want to go."

In an instant, that man got off me and ran out the door. Once I came to myself, I called the police. I was asked if I wanted to go to the hospital. My throat was hurting, red, and bruised. All I said was, "No, he is gone and I will be okay. I just need to see about my grandson and get myself together." My throat was hurting a great deal, but I heard God say, *Now I can take you higher. I can use you now, and you cannot take him back.* God was there for me the whole time.

My husband was placed in the Most Wanted ad. The police went house to house looking for him, and finally he turned himself in. I received protection orders, and the judge signed my divorce, because he had refused to divorce me but on March 10, 2010 I went to court alone and stood before the judge and he said your husband did not want to sign the papers but I will grant you a divorce and you go and be safe. I am stronger and wiser because I made it through my storm. God was there to carry me all the way. Now at this time I was alone but ok, and living alone and life could not have been better, but as the days went by changes were occurring that would lead me back in the same dark place that I was trying to get away from. I wanted to call to see how I could go about getting some burial and life insurance so I called a local funeral home and was connected to a man who was a minister that worked there. This minister I spoke with a couple of times but still had concerns about the pricing. I did not call back until a couple of weeks later and we made an appointment for him to come to my apartment but only if my sister was there because I had concerns of being with a strange man I did not know. Well the meeting was done and all went well and even got a date out of it. Before I knew it the minister and I were dating and you see my divorce was not final till the upcoming year of 2010. He was kind to me and generous and would help me when I did not even ask for it, and I was not use to a man being a man meaning giving me, taking care of me and assisting me with bills when he seen I was struggling, and that felt good. Little did I know the trap was being set in place for a letdown for me. I ended up having surgery and was planning to move from the place that I currently resided at because of the habit that was surrounding the complex, and I did no longer feel safe. Before the move I had to have surgery and was not fully able to care for myself, so he was there. When I returned home from the hospital, my electricity was off, so this man stayed and took care of me to get the lights back on. But even after that, I had to move and did not still have a clear understanding of what was happing in my life.

I should have left because the signs were staring me in the face, but I saw only what I wanted to see. I ended up having to move and had nowhere to go, and had I answered him the second week, the question he asked correctly, I would have had a place to go. I felt that at that time I did not want to move with him because I really did not know what type of man he was. He helped me move, and I ended up with temporary custody of two of my grandchildren, and it was quite hard, but we were going to make it. The children and I moved into my friend's mom's house and shared one room, but I was very appreciative of that. Still, I had a cloud of smoke over my eyes and could not see the big picture. I did not have a car or my own place, and I thought I was doing what was true in the eyes of God. The man ended up lending me his car, which was my first mistake; he also helped me with the daycare expenses and even a little more. Control was already in the progress, and it was going full speed.

I was blessed to have the mom come back into my grandchildren's' lives, but I still stayed very close to them and helped with their needs. This gave me an opportunity to move into my own place, and he helped. I was in school and working, and I ended up getting sick again and once again I had to have another surgery. He was there and paid everything for me.

I finally had to move because I could not manage the finances, and once again another surgery was approaching, and this one would keep me down for just a little bit. I ended up moving with this man because I needed help, and finally the full control came into effect. When you lose control, you are subject to fall for anything that is put before you. I should have left because the signs were staring me in the face, but again, a woman sees only what she wants to see.

Now he got full control, and I was at his mercy because I had surgery and no money, and felt that I needed him instead of depending on God. On the night after surgery, the man that I thought really cared left me at home alone, and I was not able to take care of myself. While I was down, I heard a voice tell me, *All you need is me, and if you depend on me I will take care of you. Give it to me and step back.* That is when I started trying to get my life back. I took a look at my life and began to speak these words to my Lord.

Words spoken above to God

Lord, it seems I am always in the fire. Things are hectic; I am always hit on every side with trials and temptations. I pray that I become a better person, a more faithful Christian, and a living testimony for you to show what you can do. Lord, I need you now. I need your strength. You see, I cannot do it by myself, so come on in right now and let your will be done and not mine. I will be submissive to you, Lord, so help me. I am your child, and your child is crying out to you now with open arms and stretched out to you. I give all I have and leave it with you. Bless me right now. Open my mind to your will. You be in control of me. All I need is you. The head, the middle, and the end will I forever let you be. This I ask in Jesus's name. Amen.

A Lost Son

My son was on drugs for a long time, and when I found out, it was devastating. The changes he took me through were so hard for me to understand. Not knowing the first years why he acted and treated me like he did take a great toll on me. I stuck by his side as a mother is to do for her child even when he is not doing his best. My own family members would tell me to give up on him and let him go. "He will do what he wants, and there is nothing that you can do to save him," they said. I always said to myself, God has never, nor will he ever give up on us, so why should I do that to my own son? God gives us so many chances and yet we still let him down even when he has brought us out of all the tragedies that we place ourselves in. The effect my son had on me and his two children living with him was hard to deal with, because we never knew what he was going to do. I learned feeling no love and losing someone who means a lot to you will lead you to do things that may not be of you, and you may take avenues that make you feel like you have taken a trip to space.

Psychoactive substance, more often known as psychoactive drugs, is a substance that is taken to change the thinking process. When my son used drugs, it had a great impact on his life, family, and his mind. It would alter his thinking and turn him into a violent person that he otherwise was not. The use of drugs led my son to making bad choices, living on the streets and even hiding from people. It also put him in jail because he was with the wrong people at the wrong time.

My son said and did things to me that no mother should ever have to go through, but I know it was not him; it was the drugs that took over, and I still loved my baby with all my heart. I promised myself that I would never leave his side and I would fight Satan until I got my son back from the evilness of his hands. To be cursed at and having to fight him, as well as going into spiritual battle for him, made me want to give up, but I never did. I asked God the Father to save my son. Sometimes my son would bring the kids over and would not return for days at a time. Not knowing if my child was dead or alive would keep me up at all times of the night with worry. At this time, I was still married to a man who also did drugs, lied, stole, and cheated. I wondered what I had done to deserve such misery, and I asked God to give me more than strength to get through this. After the separation and the divorce, I was left to carry the weight, and it felt as though it was getting bigger and bigger to carry, so I almost started dragging it and leaning to one side.

As a grandmother, I had to do what was right and try to accept what was going on in my life and stay strong. I had to take the kids and make sure that they were in a safe and healthy environment. One day, my son fought me because he left and I found my grandbabies with people I did not know. I did not feel right about what was being said and what I was witnessing in front of my own eyes. My son finally came to the scene, but he did not approach me in a way that a son should come to a mother. This was not my innocent son, or someone who cared about life and his family.

I remember him calling me a couple days after that incident begging for help, and, as usual, I helped him. I didn't realize it then, but I now know I was a hindrance to him. I found myself taking my grandson to and from school and picking up him and his sibling from daycare. I was raising them as though I was not just Grandmother Mimi, but mom, because their biological mother left them, leaving my son with the responsibility of raising two children on his own.

One day after leaving a hard day at work, I went home to my apartments located on the west side of Fort Worth and I began packing to move because I was not comfortable there any longer after finding out that I was not in a not-so-nice place. I felt uncomfortable because I would have several knocks on the door late at night and sometime early in the am when I was sound asleep. The apartments were full of trafficking of drugs and you could see it right in eyesight, as well as the police always chasing someone and kicking in the doors due to warrants for various reasons. I was relaxing and packing up some things, but I had a bad feeling in the pit of my stomach. Deep down inside I had a feeling that something was wrong, but I could not quite put my finger on it. Then I received a phone call. My son was on the other end, and all I heard was, "I need you, Mom. Come help me." I immediately ran out of the house with nothing but my keys and cell phone in tote, and I went looking for the unexpected, not knowing trouble was just around the bend. I did not know where he and the children were, but I saw a crowd of people, and I headed in that direction. I approached the crowd and saw my son was bleeding, but I did not see my grandbabies. I asked first, "Where are my babies?" Someone brought them to me, and I asked the young lady, "How did you get them and what in the world is going on?" I saw some people beating on my oldest son, and I called my daughter, my middle son, and the both of my boy's daddy who was trying to veer his way back into my life so he could see the grandbabies to assist me. I also called 911 and told them they needed to come. I just knew that I had God on my side as I was about to enter into battle to fight for my son as two men and a woman were fighting him. One of the men punched my son in the face as they were fighting on the way down the staircase outside from the second floor, and the grandbabies watch and crying daddy. At that moment

I ran up to assist my son as he was going down to the ground and the men trying to fight him as he fought alone with no one to help him. I looked around and seen the grandbabies as they were screaming and someone was holding onto them in the mist of the crowd outside. As I approached the man that was hitting on my son I shouted to him you will not hit him anymore or you will fight me too, and that is just what that man was about to do until I heard someone in the crowd say, "Don't anybody touch her that is his mother, and we don't know her but we will help her so keep your hands off of her and him." The police showed up but the men and the woman that was starting the altercation and fighting my son fled with no one to tell the police on the scene who they were. The ambulance came and triaged my son as well as my daughter showing up and my sons father. My son was taken by ambulance because he was bleeding from the nose which later on was broken, and the police took a report. I was told to take the children to the children's hospital because of allegation of someone fondling with my granddaughter and drugs around the children. I took the children to the pediatrics hospital in Fort Worth where CPS was called because my son the children's father had full custody of them and the allegations and the assault had occurred in front of the children. I had to answer all the questions CPS asked and testing was done on my granddaughter which later came back as negative of any issues in the manner of the baby being touched or molested. Someone said that my son sold his baby for drugs but later came back as not true by the finding of the investigation. I then received temporary custody of the children and they were placed in my home until further notice by CPS, my son was released from the hospital but could only see the children in my presence and sometimes I did not see him for days at a time, so I took care of them all on my own with the help of the current man the minister I was dating at that time.

I ended up having to raise my son's children, umm a girl who was barely one and a boy who was barely three and a half for a little bit and that altered my life a great deal. At this particular time of the ending year of 2009 at my current age of just turning forty-two and dating a man who was twenty years older, I was dating a man who helped me out so much, and I appreciated that because I was not financially able to pay for two little ones, as well as daycare. As the months and days grew long, I had to play mommy and push grandmother role to the side to give the children the love, shelter, and clothing they needed. I had custody until my son got himself together. I laid awake so many nights thinking of what went wrong and what did I do to make him go the way he did, but in the end I said it was not me; he was raised well, and it was by his choice. I knew I had to stand by him and let him know that there was a man who knew all, saw all, and would help him no matter what he had done. I said, "God, I give him back to you. I have raised him the best that I knew how, but I did not raise him to fight his mother and do drugs. I pray that you will take care of him. Several times he would show up at my door step and said he was ready, but he really was not because he would stay for a couple of days and then he would leave and you would not see him until he wanted to see you and he was really tired of being on the streets. Finally is this true is what he saying the words I wanted to hear. And the Lord did just what I had prayed for. My son came to me in the year of 2013 and said, "I need to go to a place where I can get help. I am ready. At this time his children were back with their mom whom after moving out of the apartment and having to move two times living in my best friends mom apartment to the minister I was dating before I was able to get my own apartment which was in the Meadowbrook area where at that time I did not have the children. The reason for me not having the children the court at that time felt that I should allow the mom who left them and their father having to raise them start seeing them and one day on a visit she did not return them back nor notify me but until a couple of days later saying she was going to keep her children and I will now since your son is on drugs be able to get them back with no problem. Yes that was something I wanted because

I felt that every child should be with their mom unless she is harming them or neglect. So my son understood and knew that he needed to get himself together before he end up dead or in jail so he ask to go to church with me." He went to church where I was attending in the Fort Worth area and asked for guidance and prayer, and he then went into a center to help him located on the south side of Fort Worth for a length of a year and a half. My son came to me one day and asked me to forgive him of all he had put me through and told me how much I meant to him. He said he appreciated all that I had done and now do for him in his life, and he kisses and hugs me every time we see each other. He is the son I used to have, but even better because he does know the man (God) who has stood by him the entire time.

I no longer have to fight with him; my battle was God's, and he fixed it. I no longer see my son as one of the men who hurt me. That scar is healed, and the healing process is beginning for the better. I gave it all over to God, and I stepped back and watched him work. I see the work with my own eyes. Oh how good God is to me, my son, and the family. He gave what the devil thought he could have right back to me.

When the Control of a Man Began

Women, how do we let the control we once had slip away from us so quickly without warning? Control is something we try to hold on to until we have no choice but to give it to someone. Control is not for someone to take and then try their best to run our lives, destroying it in the process. No, I will not let you have it anymore, nor will I let you take something that is not for you to take. I will no longer be weak to the point that I don't know what is happening to me. I will no longer let love blind me to the fact that it almost cost me my life, or have me fall to my knees crying, unknowing what lies ahead and unsure how to handle it. Once I had total control of my life in 1992 when I was in the process of separation from the hands of a dangerous man who took over my life and almost my soul, but that no longer is because I knew what I wanted to do and where I wanted my life to go. I knew that I wanted to be something so that I may be able to take care of the three little precious things that God blessed me with.

It was so difficult to have a man whom I loved so much and gave part of myself to shatter it all within a year's time. God, where did I go wrong and how did I let that wall that I thought I would never let down fall so quickly. To destroy me, kill me, batter me, and abuse me was something that came once the control took place. How can a man who says he cares mistreat someone so wrong? To try to take over someone because you do small things for them even the large things does not give you the reason to control that person. I lost the control when I let my guard down, not thinking and not asking God what I should do and how I should handle what is put before me. Just because you fall does not give a person the opportunity to take over. Yes, I lost control, and I had to decide, *do I let this continue to happen, or do I take my life back?* I will not allow any man to have that much control over me again regardless of my situation. The only man who has control is the man named Jesus.

After the separation and the devastation I went through I finally started to gain my life back. Previously I went through a relationship that I thought would last forever when I married my first husband who was the father of my two sons, but that was not so. I got into a relationship that I thought was the right thing for me, and yes, I even prayed. Now I wonder, did the real answer come from God or did I just hear what I thought I wanted to hear?

After going on into the relationship, I saw some signs but I just pushed them to the side. I thought it would be right this time. The reason I thought this was different was because he was a man that gave me so much of himself and his time, and I knew that he just knew how to treat a woman. Once again, I learned that it does not matter if he is a man in the will of God or a man on the streets he is still a man, and see this man was raised in church. This particular man had me see that all men cannot be trusted. When did I lose the control I had? Was I blind to love and quick to make it work? Just because a man says thank you, Jesus, and speaks a great word does not mean he is for you. You must always give it to God in prayer, step back, and watch, look, and listen.

Not realizing what was in front of me, I went in with a mind closed and I let my guard down. I lost control very quickly, and he took it and ran. When a man thinks he can, he will; and if you don't realize it, he will take control and hold onto it as long as he can until you come to the knowledge of what he is doing.

The control that I once gave or let someone take was stolen from me within a blink of an eye. I now have it back, and oh how wonderful I feel knowing that I am somebody and I can do all things through Christ who gives me strength.

I will be able to leave here and not have to return again with the Lord on my side, I will and can take it all back. That full and complete control.

Man is This?

On June 9, 2012, I had a time with a man who I really thought cared for me. This man would lie to me and hide things from me that you would not even believe, and sometimes I would fall for all of it.

I remember a stupid incident happened, and he tried to turn it back on me and make me feel like I was the crazy one. He called the police on me because I did not move my car so that he could park his car in the garage. He had washed off his tires and was taking his car to the car wash, and he came in and said some ugly things to me.

He went to the car wash, so I moved my car over to be able to reach the water hose and wash my own vehicle. I was not in the space too long, and I had started washing the car. It was soaped down, and I had gotten myself all wet when he came around the corner and demanded that I move my car. He wanted me to move my car right away and do what he was telling me to. If I didn't, I would suffer. He jumped out of his car and demanded that I move at once. I said, "I do not do you like that. I make sure you are taken care of and try to make you happy, but am I really happy with myself and this relationship? Is it healthy, or is it meant for bad?" I asked him to leave me alone and let me finish and quit following me around the car like a two-year-old.

He then called the Desoto Police on me and told them that I was causing domestic violence, and he needed some help because

I was in his face and he needed to have me removed from his place. I had my God brother on the line, because if something happened he would know and could assist if needed. The police came and said to him, "Did she hit you?" He told them yes, and they asked me to come over to the side and speak with them. The police then asked him, "Sir, does she stay here with you?" He told them that I did not stay there and that I was just a friend who was visiting. They asked me, "What are you to him?" I explained and showed them my driver's license, and it had the address of the place that I had my feet planted on. Why did this man try to get me in trouble with the law when I had not done anything wrong? They asked me to move the car so it would make him feel better, even though it was stupid and childish. I said okay to keep down confusion, and I did so.

While I was outside and alone, I finished washing my car. I was talking to God and told him my mind was full and confused, and I needed complete guidance. *Please help me, because I really don't think this man cares for me. I think he is really out to get what he can for only himself. God, I know that this is not the place for me and that you will take me where I need to be if I just let you, but I keep telling myself he will change, and I do love and care for him. I thought that when I asked for a man of God you gave me this man, but did you really give him to me and does he really have God in him?*

A Man of Explosion

I sit outside in the dark, gazing at what I think I see, not realizing it really isn't dark; just sitting next to a man of explosion is whom I see. Behind the expensive suits, the cocky style, the cologne, and the fake smile is a bomb waiting to explode. Behind the tears, fear, and disappointments there lies a man who feels like he will never win. Behind the lies that people have placed on you, there stands a man who seems to never give up, but the enemy stills hits him harder and harder than ever. This is why I call you a man of explosion. Behind the lies one after another, there lies a man who is unsure of himself. Behind the degrees and knowledge, there is still yet some type of determination and hope, and yet still there is a man with a great explosion.

Matthew 21:22 states if you believe you will receive whatever you ask in prayer

Proverbs 16:9 in his heart a man plan his course but the Lord determines his course

Somewhere along the way, Man of God, you veered off, so come back to your first love that you know, and every door that He has closed He will surely open. Stop lying to women and even yourself. God sees and hears all that we do. This goes out to the man of explosion.

Somewhere in life, your pride was broke in two and your heart was hurt, so now without knowledge hurt the ones who really love you. Love. Do you really know what that means? Or can you only truly tell others but not yourself? Love goes further than one can imagine, and only God has that true Love for us all.

Behind the secrets you hide, you want to reveal sometimes, so that you can be free of yourself. You say things to make others feel that they are beneath you, man of explosion. There is no habit that God can't change, and I know you can if you want to. The hiding of other women you did from the lady that loves you the most, but my Father whom sits high and looks low sees all and one day bring it to an open shame. You too can change for the better, man of explosion. Saying one thing to one woman and lying to another, making her think she is dumb, is something you too can change.

If you don't want what is there, then be truthful to yourself before you explode on the innocent. Time will tell if you are true to yourself, your woman, and most of all God.

Put it in God's hand and let go of all the issues that have, had, and may occur. There is nothing too hard for God and you know that by ministering on a daily, and if you truly repent of all your wrong doing and mean it from your heart man of God. The dirty mind that you try to hide from others, but you can't because what is dominated in you will surely come out when you meet others because they will be able to see right through the explosion meaning the danger you hold within.

I will leave you for right now, but I was told to tell you to give up let go and repent and start this new year off with a right mind and love the one who loves you. Hugs and kisses go a long way.

Before you explode, release it all to God.

***

Any way you bless me, Lord, I will be satisfied. See, I know it is truly my blessing that is on the way. Looking for love in all the wrong places was all I was doing. But when I truly found you, you heard my cry and were right there by my side. He was wounded for my transgression and bruised for my inequities. See, all I do know is that by his stripes I am healed. Faithful and grateful I am. See? Yes, God has it all in control, just hold on and enjoy the ride.

Materialistic Man of God

(A man I once dated)

Materialistic man of God, you know who you are. A man who thinks that without the big fine house, the Benz, the gold and silver, you have nothing. Materialistic man of God, without the fine cologne, the elk skin shoes, and the embroidered handkerchief, you think you have nothing. Materialistic man of God, you think it is all about having the biggest TV and a lot of bathrooms in your home. Materialistic man of God, how well do you really see life for what it is, and how do you really look at others? No, not being judgmental of others but stepping back and focusing on what and where God wants to take you.
It is not what you have in your house and what type of vehicle you drive and how many suits you have in your closets. It is God who is all you need. Stop and see what I see; it is all about the true Man—the man who loves you for not what you have how much money you have in the bank, but what is deep within your heart.
I believe that if you push all things aside and focus on what is set before you and ask God to guide you, he will see you through.

Speak to Me

Tell me who can make a mountain move out of my way. Who can make the rivers calm and behave? Who can bring joy to everyone and can calm a roaring storm? His name is Jesus the Son of God.

Tell me who can move the pain that runs so deep in me within my veins. Who can bring such joy when there is pain? I need and want to be free.

Oh, His name is Jesus, Jesus, Jesus the Lilly of the valley, bright as the morning star, and nobody but Jesus can fill this empty void.

As a woman, I will give my all and all to be what He wants me to be. During the cries, the sorrow, and all of the pain, I will make and can make it when I give it to God and don't worry about anything, nor will I complain.

So put it on the altar and watch and see how prayer changes things. No more worrying and crying, just know that you are never alone, because Jesus is our friend, and He knows all about what we are going through, have been through and will go through.

Nobody but Jesus will be there for us in all that we go through. He will never leave us nor forsake us, so speak to me, Lord, and I will forever answer your call. Speak to my heart, speak to my mind, and fill my soul with everlasting gain. I need you to speak to me as long as I am in the land of the living and tell me what I need to do. Speak to me and tell me what to do; speak to my feet, and I will watch them walk with me and lead me in the right direction. Speak to my hands and let them make a loud noise so that everyone can hear a song of praise from on high. Speak to me, Lord, and tell me what to do, and I will go and run when you call. Speak to me, Lord, yes I will hear you and answer when you call. Oh, how happy I will be when I can stand tall for my Jesus. Yes, I will wait for you to call, and I will answer. Speak, Lord, and yes I will wait for you to call.

When God Chose Me

I never knew nor did I understand the reason anyone was chosen by God and why. I would hear many say, "You can't just pick yourself; He picks you." I asked who sometimes when and why? How do you know when you are chosen for what He has for you to do? Yes, everyone is to go out and tell people of the goodness and greatness of Jesus and how you can be saved, and yes He did die for all of us. How do you know what your calling is, and do you get it at a certain age or a certain time of the year?

Chosen to take as a choice; select. To decide or prefer. These are the words from Webster's New World Dictionary

I went to a pastor one time, and he said that yes, God chooses certain people to be called to a higher standard, and we must answer his call or take what may lie ahead until you decide to let Jesus have you totally mind, body, and soul. I asked, does he send you a sign, and if so what kind of sign do you look for? This man of God told me that there is a divine spirit, and you will then know when you feel and hear it.

I knew that I was very different from others. I could feel and see things that I thought to myself, *I know that I am an amazing young lady gifted and full of God's power, and I must let God use me to be open to his will. God has not given up on me, and I will not give up on him, for he has something that I must go through and complete.*

I was born from my mother's womb full of sin. I have learned that I must be going through and have been through many difficult seasons in my life, and oh by the grace and mercy of God I was carried through. I would lie awake at night and wonder why I was going through this and where was God when I truly needed Him. I would see visions and never knew what they meant until one day I heard Him with a great voice say my name as though another human was in the room with me. I heard it again as I felt a soft touch, which was hard for me because I knew I was the only one in the room. *Tonya*, the voice called out again. I ignored it and went on my way, saying to myself, I must be going crazy, because I was very young at that time—around ten years old—when I first heard it, and still one day when I was older I heard it again.

One day the storms felt as though they were raging in my life, and I could not take what I was going through. I fell down to my knees and said, *Lord, if you want me to go, I will surely go.* Then once I arose, I knew that when I said yes, He hid me; hid me so close Him as though I was right there with Him. Ever since then, I got up and have been running for Him all the way regardless of the storms, and oh how the winds blew. I made it and I am still going on.

I was chosen to do His will, and that I will do to the fullest. I was chosen by my Father to go on regardless how hard and how many storms may blow my way. How many mountains I must have to climb and how many valleys I may have to go through. Regardless of the tears that fall during the day as well as the night, I was chosen. By the mercy and grace, He will give to me as I do His will. I will not fight my Lord; I will just continue until this race is run in full. For I know that He will never leave me nor forsake me. Yes, my Lord, I will go to the highways and the byways and tell everyone the goodness you can and will do for your children if we just let go and let God have His way. I was chosen for a great journey just to be able to tell how He has brought me out, and He will do the same for you. I will trust

God in everything that He will take me through. I was chosen by my Lord, and I am excited to keep going on and watch and see what lies ahead for me. There will be glory after this.

When the Storms are Raging in My Life

When the storms are raging in my life like a ship out on a sea while the waters roar, I will stand firm to the word. When it seems like I cannot see my way out and the tide grows high, I will pray until I get a breakthrough. Like the trees when the leaves fall off during a hurricane, I feel my life is the same way, and I will give it all to God. And when I feel like giving up, I will call on the Lord, and He will supply all my needs according to His will.

When the storms of life are raging, stand by me, Lord. When it seems as though my life is tossed and torn, stand by me. When my friends forsake me and it seems as though family is few, Lord, oh Lord, I need you to stand by me.

Stand by me, Lord, as the woman that I am. Help me to be strong with all that I have to go through. Help me to be the woman of God that you called me to be—the mother, sister, daughter, friend, goddaughter, and granddaughter. Lord, raise me up to be that strong and powerful woman. Help me to make it through this stormy sea of life. Raise me up to be more than what I see. Raise me up through this raging sea. Though the pillars toss, and I feel torn, oh yes, I have made many mistakes in my life, but I do know that you have forgiven and thrown it into the sea, never to return again.

So as the seas keep raging, and my life is filled with ups and down. I know, oh how I know you have been there for me the whole time.

Yes, the storms will keep on raging as long as I shall live, but I do know there is a man who sits high and looks low and will tackle every storm that comes my way if I just climb into the boat with Him and let Him be the captain of that ride.

Now ride on, woman of God, ride on into what He has for you to do and know that He is the captain and you are the mate. So, mate, do as His will says. If you have to throw Him your paddles and let Him just guide you to that great place, don't tug on the line, just untie and let the captain glide you safety. So lie down and go to sleep, mate, and know that the boat's captain has it all under control. He will guide you to a place where you will never want for more.

The Move that Broke the Chains

When you start looking at life and trying to measure good and the bad, you sometimes get amazed by what is revealed to you. Thinking that you possibly know someone tends to channel down a dark and cold road. As I started pondering my life because of the turmoil that I was facing on a daily basis, I came across something that would change the course of my life forever. The man the minister the one who calls himself a great Christian man the one who I was living with but not married almost drove me to losing my mind. If I came home anywhere after eight o'clock, that was considered late, and I was in wrongdoing. I was trying to receive my associate's degree in paralegal, starting in 2012 and graduating in January 2013 at the age of forty- four as I was scheduled for ground classes, which were out at a certain time, and I would have to drive a distance to where I was living. This would have me entering the house sometimes around 10:30 p.m.

This man tried to break me by way of physical and mental abuse. This man thought that he could break me to the point of no return. He fought me when and if I did something he did not like, and the actual fighting was not often; it was more mental, and he tried to take me to a point where I thought that I was a nobody. He tried to break my pride and dignity. He tried to take me down and bring me to my knees every day, but, in reality, it was hard for him because I kept fighting back each day. When he saw that he could not break me, he kept on until he did something that no one, not even a man who stated he held a high title in the church, would do and while I was at work making a daily living he threw me out in the cold.

I left home around 6:30 a.m. after the early-morning speaking with him about him still engaging with his ex-wife. The night before, she had called. He answered, and I heard her voice. I went to bed and told him that I would not worry about anything because what lies in the dark would come to the light. It is always revealed, and there will be consequences behind every action. I woke for work, singing and praising as always, and giving God the glory just to be alive another day as I walked in the room where he was. I told him to have a blessed day, not knowing that my world was about to turn upside down, and I would need God to see me through all that I was about to endure.

See, when people plot and scheme to hurt you, sometimes it works out for your good, and God will get all the glory from it. How could I be delivered if I was still in the fire? I had to come out, but not with my help, it had to be the help of the Lord, my God, who would bring me through it all.

I did not know that the entire day while I was at work, this man was moving my items that he only wanted me to have into storage and taking what he wanted of mine later to make sure he still had ties to be able to contact me. Instead of calling me to inform me I must go and doing it the correct way by the law or even giving me some time to get some money together to be able to move, he showed the coward man in him and took what he wanted of mine. This man had decided that he would still be in control of me no matter what I said or thought. As the day ended, I did not know that I was on my way to a Christmas party, but I ended up having a sick feeling that I could not shake off. I traveled home to a house that I was not to be able to get in anymore because of his evil doing. I was unaware that when I approached the house, I would not be able to enter because he had changed the code to the garage. See, I did not realize that I had a week ago asked God to do something for me and meant exactly what I said when I did. "God," I stated, "if it is your will, please remove me from the wrong issues in my life. If this man is not for me, please remove the man or remove me from the man. Anything that is not like you, remove me right now, but cause no harm to the man, and let me be safe when you do so." If I let God do it, then I would not be able to go back to the situation, and I would be able to move in peace.

He had given his daughter and her cousins instructions to hurt me, if necessary, if I tried to get into the house. He also told them to tell the police that I never lived at the house. When the police came, I told them that I did stay there, and they asked me for my driver's license, and the address matched the address to the house. She told the police that I never lived there and had not been at that residence in a long time. The police told me that I should call the constable.

I was able to speak with the man of God on the phone that I was living with but now no longer staying in the same house under the same roof because he had thrown me out, said to me "You had a big house to stay in, but you choose to hang around family and friends. You wanted to talk to your god brother and sister, your pastor, and get counseling from the church, so go and live with all of them and let them take care of you like I did. If you would have done what I said and shut up and be quiet and don't say anything about what I do or what goes on, you could have stayed here and not worried about any bills. You need to learn to shut up and do as you are told."

But the woman that God made me could no longer take the abuse that was dished out to me. This took a great toll on me, and I cried for some days without eating. Going to seek counseling is what I had to do because I did not have trust in man anymore, nor did I have trust in a man of God, one who said he was called to preach and teach God's uncompromising word. Learning that you asked the Father up above who art in heaven who knows what is best for you and that he will always provide and see you through something is what I had to do quick, fast, and in a hurry, because I was seeing myself go by the wayside, and that is not what the Father above wanted me to do. God did not want me to give up He wanted me to let go give all my problems to Him and just hold on.

"Hold on, Tonya, I am in control if you allow me to be, and I will take care of you. Let me work this out because I have a plan and a destiny in your life that I need you to do. I will not leave you, nor forsake you. I have done what I had already intended to do, so allow me to continue and give it all to me."

I realized that God had just released me from jail, and jail is where I felt like I was with shackles on hands and feet. He had broken me free from the guard who was in control of my life and all that I allowed him to do. I was free, and the chains were no longer on my wrists, and the shackles were no longer on my ankles. That felt wonderful—something I had not felt in a long time. God set me free, so now I could walk into what he had for me. I said yes, giving all I had. Yes, Lord, I will allow you to do your will, and I will allow you to let me go through what you need to do, and I will journey through the rough times, and you will get all of the glory for what you have done for me, what you brought me through, and how I made it over. Set me free is what he did. I can enjoy life as God wants me to, and minister to all who have been in bondage and tied up for so many years. Our father does not want us to live in misery and pain; he wants us to rely on him and call on him, and he will bring us through and supply all of our needs according to his will.

God has a purpose and a plan for you, and you must allow Him to guide you through it all. Walk into what is granted for you and hold on and enjoy the ride, which will be smooth if you let God be the driver and you stay the passenger. Let no man control nor dictate what you can and can't do for yourself or for your family. Break those chains that are so easily bestowed on you, and don't be tied down to things that are not like God. God has always had a master plan for you, but sometimes we veer onto a different path and think that we have it all under control. But it will soon let us know that the Lord is truly in control. Know that in the end, when all the chains have fallen off and you are able to enjoy what God has for you, it will feel just like heaven has opened all doors and peace has truly entered in. I used to wonder what was going to happen if I was all alone with nowhere to go and no one to turn to, and what I would have to face with the entire problem that weighs on my mind and shoulders. Thinking I can handle it all; I can do this by myself. In the end, I was not even strong enough to do anything. Even though the tears fell and it seemed I couldn't see my way out and nobody cared, I had to say to myself, "Just hold on, because my God has all the answers to that entire question that you don't even understand. God will fix it, Tonya, hold on. You have been scorned, but you have not been broken. I have a plan for you—a path that you must journey, and though you may feel like giving up, hold on. God will see me through. He holds the key to life, and he keeps a tight grip on it in his hands, and he does not let go."

The chains are now broken, so walk into what God has for you. Know the doors will open, and you will find me. Love and peace that you thought was gone really never left. The Lord says that he has never left you and has been carrying you all the way. No more bondage, shackles, no chains holding you back from the destiny he has provided. Walk into victory, for the Lord has set you free.

Scorned but not broken, a great woman of God. Although the pain is so great and the tears flow, you are a stronger woman to stand tall and firm. With God's loving grace and his mercy, I will stand tall and rise to the occasion of peace and know all I have been through was only a test. I was scorned, but I am not broken because God held the key to my life and keeps me afloat and keeps me going to move on another day. A day of peace and tranquility, love comfort, and joy. No longer am I in your prison anymore, because I am free. I am strong and confident knowing that with God's help I will make it through, and in the end I will be victorious with the help of the Lord. Scorned but not broken, I will rise.

Learning to live again

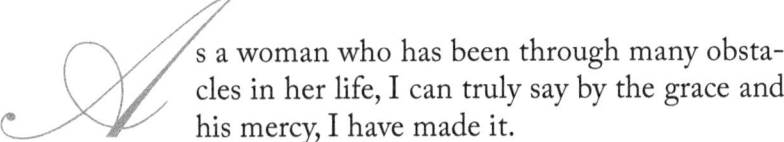

As a woman who has been through many obstacles in her life, I can truly say by the grace and his mercy, I have made it.

I no longer live in the past, for the past is just what it is—in the past. Not to return nor look back like Lot's wife did as she turned into a pillar of salt.

When we say the past is the past, we should never allow ourselves or anyone to take us back there; that is what we sometimes allow others to do to us, as well as ourselves. Allowing this to happen means that we have let someone control us, and we are not able to let God have his way.

So as you move forward, you learn to live regardless of the pain, temptation, regret, fear, and even the abuse that was endured by the man whom you loved, family, and even so-called friends.

In moving on you learn to live and take one day at a time because each day is different, and we do not know what that day may hold for us until we reach it. Only the Father up above knows what that day may hold, and so we must rely on him to help us make it through.

You learn that even though you have scars you can be healed and live past the scars, hurt, and the pain. Now we say scars, which we know may vary considering, we have scars of many types. There are emotional, physical, and psychological scars, and even the scars of a tragic aftermath of losing a loved one.

We also have a scar of loneliness, lost opportunities, and even abandonment.

In order to live again and live past the hurt and the pain, you must recognize and realize that yes, I have been hurt and through the hurt I will live. Hurt is an inescapable part of everyday life that we sometimes endure on an everyday basis. The only problem we have is when we let the pain of the hurt take over or control the way we live and shatter our faith and the hope we may have for a great future.

Our father in heaven always wants to welcome us to Him. Jesus stated in Matthew 28:20 NIV "Surely I am with you always, to the very end of the age." Giving it to God is the big step in order to live and be free of the worrying and fear that will try to take over a woman who has been scorned. Give it to God, leave it, and do not go back and pick it up, which I used to do over and over. God sees all and knows all, so He wants us to come to Him with an open heart and open mind and trust and believe that He can and will if we let Him help us to overcome and live again.

God looks and waits for us to come to Him. He is knocking, so open up and let Him come into your life. God deserves to embrace you, to hold you, and shower you with all the love and compassion. God will love you like no one has ever loved you, and he will restore you and freely give us everything we need to help us to become all that He desires us to be and to have.

Women, let us not be like the widow in the Old Testament who gave up on hope because she felt that there was no need for her to live after going through a tragic encounter.

1 Kings 17:7-12

And it happened after a while that the brook dried up, because there had been no rain in the land. Then the word of the Lord came to him, saying, "Arise, go to Zarephath, and when he came to the gate of the city, indeed a widow was there gathering sticks. And he called to her and said, "Please bring me a little water in a cup that I may drink." And as she was going to get it, he called to her and said, "Please bring me a morsel of bread in your hand." Then she said, "As the Lord your God lives, I do not have bread, only a handful of flour in a bin, and a little oil in a jar; and see, I am gathering a couple of sticks that I may go in and prepare it for myself and my son, that we may eat it, and die.

Now we must break all ties to misery and know that God has promised to provide for our needs; by the power of God we can become self-sufficient. Our lives can change by our revelation of what we allow God to desire to do in our lives. We do know and understand that we overcome and are delivered in one area of our life another challenge will occur, and that is when if we want to live and more efficient in what God have for us to do, we will continue to let go and let God.

Learning to live again is a big challenge within itself. I had to let go and let God through all that I have encountered I had to step back several feet and take a big picture and evaluate the situation at hand. Can I do this by myself, or is there something or somebody that I can turn to for help and who will not ridicule me again? I needed help, and I had to rely solely on God and no one else.

In order for me to live, I had to learn to forgive and forget and throw it into the pool of forgiveness. Not to bring it back up meant I had to forget it and not let anyone who was tied to me bring up any negative things that may have occurred in my life. You hear them say you can forgive but not forget. That is wrong. In order for me to live again and be complete with myself and to God, in order for me to heal and go through the next chapter and receive my blessing, I had to do both. Though the scars were there, the healing process had to take place once I uncovered it and let it heal correctly.

I once spoke to my daughter and my son on the same day I was going through something, and found that they understood and received what I told them and they had to give me back my own advice. You think that children don't listen, but later on down the line you will be able to see the great results about what was held in their mind when you told them.

"Momma," my oldest son stated to me. "Though they called me a crack head and said that I was nothing, I heard and I know God lives, so I will give you back your own advice and forgive and forget what was done to you and just move on. In order for you to get what God has for you, forget so you can fully close that chapter in your life. You told us that everybody will not treat you like you treat them, but God has a blessing for you, and you must be able to receive what it is fully. So let it go, as you say."

That was my son, whom I had been praying for and who should have died six times. But in God's mercy and His grace, I thank Him for each and every day. The child that I had to chase, get talked to bad, run and save from danger on numerous occasions, gave me my own words of encouragement that I once told him. My heart filled with tears as I heard him speak those words and then tell me *God is not through with you.* I prayed and prayed for him as well as my other son and daughter as we were going through our hard time, and now I have been blessed to pray for my grandchildren who are in my life now, which is a great blessing to see.

I am learning to live again and call on the name of Jesus Christ. I want to be able to see heaven one day. I want to be able to see my loved ones who have gone on before me. I don't want anything I do to be done in vein. I will put my entire problem on the altar and leave it there, because it is not mine it is the Lord's. Prayer changes things, and if I want to live a life that God has promised me, I need to give him *all* of my burdens and leave them, not to pick them up. Whether the problem is too small or too big, it is not mine to deal, with so I pray and give it to God and step back and watch what He can do. Free of worrying and knowing that God has it all in control, not to say that Satan will not try to come in when he sees that everything is going okay for you, because that is his job to rob, kill, and destroy. So your big defense is God. If you are sick and tired of the stress, give it to Him and watch. Put them all on the altar and when you get off your knees leave it there.

(Nahum 1:3-5)
The Lord has His way In the whirlwind and in the storm, And the clouds are the dust of His feet. He rebukes the sea and makes it dry, And dries up all the rivers. Bashan and Carmel wither, And the flower of Lebanon wilts. And the flower of Lebanon wilts. The mountain quake before Him, The hills melt, And the earth heaves at His presence, Yes the world and all and all who dwell in it.

(Nahum 1:7)
The Lord is good, A stronghold in the day of trouble; And He knows those who trust in Him

(John 14:27)
Peace I leave with you, My peace I give to you; not as the world gives do I give to you. Let not your heart be troubled, neither let it be afraid.

So when you have done all that you know how and all you want to do is live and not give up give it to God and know He is the Alpha the Omega the beginning and the end. He can do all things in your favor if you allow Him to do so. Say this and mean it with all your heart because this has helped me on a daily basis to live more and more each day when the troubles of this old world seem to weigh me and toil on my every being.

Ps 138:3
In the day when I cried out, You answered me, and made me bold with strength in my soul

Is 41:10

> *Fear not, for I am with you; be not dismayed, for I am you God. I will strengthen you. Yes I will help you, I will uphold you with My righteous right hand*
> **Ps 30:5**
> *For His anger is but for a moment, His favor is for life; weeping may endure for a night, but joy comes in the morning*
> **Ps 138:7**
> *Though I walk in the midst of trouble, You will revive me; You will stretch out Your hand against the wrath of my enemies, and Your right hand will save me*
> Matt 5:44
> But I say to you, love your enemies, bless those who curse you, do good to those who hate you, and pray for those who spitefully use you and persecute you
> Ps 27:14
> Wait on the Lord; be of good courage, and He shall strengthen your heart; wait, I say on the Lord

So when you feel embarrassed, empty, threatened, tempted, troubled, sad, lonely, discouraged, depressed, confused, angry, afraid, like giving up, hurt, hopeless, troubled, weak, weary, and worried; When you need money, knowledge, love, peace, safety, patience, when you need to forget, face doubts, need strength, face failure, family troubles, when you face heartbreak, grief, when you face misunderstandings, face sickness or even separation I need you to know in order to live again you should go to the word. That simple little book that everyone tries to ignore, sitting there on your bookshelf when you want to live, pick it up, pray, and ask God to help you in your situation, whatever the circumstance may be. Within the Bible you find power, authority, dependable, a healer, a resource, protection, and security.

We need healing in order for us to live again, and healing comes from Christ. Christ holds all the power in his hands; God who created us wants us to be set free, so we must realize that if you diligently heed to the voice when He calls, fall on your knees and say, Lord, you are all I have and all that I need. Help me.

Change me, Lord, touch my mind, body, and soul. Give me the peace and take all this that I hold; it is yours, and help me to live again. Free from all hurt, harm, and danger.

If we keep all His commandments and obey His laws and ask God to empty that vessel and put into me what you have me to do, use me, Lord. I believe the divine healing will come in, and I will be able to be free to go do your will. Let flesh die whether it is the adultery, fornication, uncleanness, licentiousness, idolatry, jealousies, or hatred. I want to have that one on one relationship with you, God, so that you may work fully in my life that I may live. Live with love, peace, longsuffering, kindness, self-control, gentleness, and faithfulness.

1 Cor 13:13
And now abide faith, hope, love, these three;
but the greatest of these is love
1 Peter 2:2
So let live so that we may go out and do the works that are ask of us to do. We have to live so that we may be witness of Jesus to others. So now you don't have to live with the guilt because it is gone and you have been forgiven of your sins and now you must live to do the work according to God. We learn to grow in grace and in knowledge of the things of God
2 Peter 3:18
We grow as we read the word

We are living to serve, not just to sit on our hinny and do nothing. The Christian life is like a roller coaster—you either go on or endure the ups and downs, the hills, the slope and the curves, or you get off and enjoy what the world has to offer with no hope, guidance, or even a covering of protection. We live in a world of beginnings and endings, and in the end where do we want to be.

I am learning to live again because I want to hear Him say, "You can come on in." I want to make it to heaven and get my reward; just to even get in the gate is really all I want. I don't need a big mansion, I just want to see Jesus and hear Him say, "Well done, my good and faithful servant. To live again is to gain victory, and I so want to see those streets that are made of gold, the half has not even been told. I do not want my living to be in vain, so I must do the work down here that He wants me to do so that I can take Him by the hand and be able to see Him face to face. Just to live is a wonderful thing if you know Jesus and accept Him as your Lord and Savior. Life is adventurous and everlasting.

If Only You Could Know

Everything was so peaceful; it was such a beautiful night
Things were going extremely well, I was
a woman who enjoyed her flight
The symmetry and geometry of my mind, life had
no room for any distortion or destruction
You've been blessed with a great gift from
above and great gift from God.
Yes, a chosen one
Embrace what is to become; sit back in awe
The graceful heavy things that were in my past that
no one could have ever imaged took a great toll on
me and almost brought me down to my knees
As I slowly undress each bitter crisis that was placed
in my life, all I wanted was just for the feeling and
pain to go away without misery and strife
I savor the moments that I have now, which I could now explain with great joy in my voice. I desire you, Lord, and know that you will truly lead me in the way that I need to go. I will continue to explore each and every moment, taking it slowly with my hands reaching out to you and with my voice I will sing your praises. I will get on board and take the adventurous ride and love every moment as though I was on a giant rollercoaster at high speed even cloud nine. Your strength and your love will keep me secure, and your love will keep me on the right path that I should go when I veer off to another direction. If there is any way that you tell me to go

and I happen not to, push me, pick me up, guide me, and yes speak to me, and I will do as I am told, because the love you have shown me and where you have brought me is something that no man nor anyone could have or will know. This love is unconditional love. It is not like any other love that I have ever known. If only you could know, and I do know now you do. You knew all along, because Jesus, it was always you.

Imagine

To imagine is picturing something that I love and cherish being next to me. Some say imagine is to believe something that is unreal and not true, but I say my Father is not just my imagination, but someone who is truly real to me.

The man who sits high on the throne and looks low, and supplies all my needs according to his will is not a dream to me. No I don't imagine that; it is real.

Lord, I never could have imagined that things could be so good with you here in my life. Without you here, my world would be turned upside down. I never thought that my life would go so smoothly when I gave it all over to you. My heart, mind, body, and my soul all belong to you.

The grace of an eagle on his daily flight as it is traveling through many obstacles and turbulence on its journey with no concerns is what I feel when I imagine. No concerns, it says, soaring through the sky, imagining that the Lord is his protector and if he should fall he will catch you and bring you back to him safely. Smooth sailing is what I would want like the eagle when he is on his flight, and that is what I imagine all the time with you, Lord, in my life.

Lord, I ask that your loving arms protect me through the night and the day. Carry me on the safe and narrow way as you have done so far, leading me, guiding me, and protecting me is what I imagine from you.

Imagining you not being in my life is something that I don't take lightly. Imagining not being able to talk with you, feeling you, and having that comfort from you would take me to a level that I dare not go.

Lord, I want to know if this is real and not me imagining this in my mind, so please show me a sign so I'll know that it's real all the time from up above that I might know it's your love.

I never could imagine that things could be so real without you here in my life, and I never thought they would be so perfect with your tender, precious, and wonderful grace, which sends me flying on a spiritual high.

No More Tears on My Pillow

Now I lay me down to sleep, I would always pray to the Lord my soul to keep. If I should cry while I am awake and even in my sleep, I always pray to the Lord my soul he would always keep.

My pillowcase holding my favorite pillow inside was soaked from all the tears that I would cry. As I placed my head down and my heart filled with sorrow and my body tensed, I began to weep, and then the tears would flow down my face and hit my pillow and sometimes even my sheets. Why, Lord, did I do this to myself? Why did I not give it to you so I would not feel this way? Help me, Lord, not to shed another tear—not tears of fear and hurt, but tears of joy.

As I used to lie in my bed on my pillow with my eyes focusing on the ceiling, my heart pounding and my chest throbbing with pain, my eyes would well with tears—not tears of joy, but tears of pain. I ask to the Lord above, can you please help me to stop these tears that flow from my eyes onto my pillow, and can you ease the pain? The Lord catches each one as they trickle down my face and soak my pillowcase. I pray to my father above, if you can hear me, please help me not to cry anymore so I won't have to keep turning this pillow over, which is drenched with my tears from a man whom I once loved and who hurt me so badly.

As I focused on the Lord as the days went by, learning how to depend on him, my tears stopped. Oh, Father, I know in my heart now that you are able to catch me when I fall and even when I cry. No more crying for the man who tried to put me to death. The Lord has your back and will catch every last one when your tears they fall. No more tears on my pillow, I heard him say, because, my child, I have wiped every last one of them away with the handkerchief of my love. So not any more tears. See, tears of joy from a man who sits high on the throne and will take care of all my needs. A man I now will cry for who shows me love and gives me peace within myself and in my heart. That will be the man I will have tears of joy for. This man is Jesus my Lord and my Savior who died for you as well for me and rose to save us all. Give it to him, and when you should fall, call on him and he will see you through it all.

So no more tears for you, Tonya, because you gave all the pain and the sorrow to the man who holds tomorrow. The cries now will be for my Jesus because he will help me through it all; he is the one who will not let me fall. So dry up those tears, my sister, and give him a call. When you call, you will see the tears disappear and no longer fall. For the Father will catch and hold each one in the palm of his hand and then keep you from falling in life's sinking sand. So we say, women, no more tears to fall. Fall no more on my pillow as I call. Father, hold me as I sleep; cover me, shield and protect me so I will no longer fall into the sorrow of tears that hit my pillow for I truly give it all to you.

God Can

"Comfort to women"
Woman, I know that God can if we just let Him. I know the pain is so deep that you sometimes feel no one can truly understand what you are going through. I know the sorrow is so heavy that your heart feels like bricks are lying on top.

The tears you cry, He has and will catch every one, and you wonder why I have not seen them fall. Just know that He is a man who sits high and looks low, and He will take care of that pain, take over the sorrow, and dry your eyes. I will not shed another tear. That is what I said to myself many months ago, but oh, how I was so wrong. When I thought it was over, it felt as it was starting all over again. I don't want to feel lonely, nor do I want to be hurt, so Father, I know you hear me when I call. Help me is all I can say.

As the strong woman I know I am, please help me to find myself, which I feel is buried so deep down inside of me. Help me to find that beautiful, vibrant young lady that you made me and find that smile that was there only to be replaced with a frown.

Hold me in your arms and rock me to sleep, for the rest is needed so that I may be whole again. I want to feel the love that I once felt and have the smile that would brighten up a room when I walked in. I want to have that sweet confidence about myself and to keep my head held high. That is what I want. I know that He can because He done it before. I know that He can, and He will if I just believe in my heart and watch the miracles that He can perform in my life just like He did many years ago.

I was placed in a basket like baby Moses and floated down the river to be placed into a house to be taken care of. Taken care of by a man who doesn't even know that I was sent there to be healed, and healed I will be. I was sent here to a certain man's house the ministers house, so that I will be able to go through the many tests that God had placed upon me. Only to be able to come out with victory and control I will defeat this. Yes, I was placed in Pharaoh's house to get stronger and wiser to all that is to be put before me so that I may be able to be a help to many others who will need to seek Jesus. See, He can and has always been there even when I thought I was about to lose my mind. He can because as the sun shines in the east, it will also shine in the west. Knowing that He will, He can, and He is able to do all things I will be a strong, independent, vibrant, loving, gentle, kind-hearted, God-fearing woman. I am a woman who has had many ups and downs, many challenges and many dark roads but made it through. I was taught that there is a price to pay for all that you go through, and your reward you will seek if you can run the race that is set before you. Woman, don't give up in all you do because God will surely see you through. Baby Moses grew up to do the will of our God and just like Moses did I will too. Don't give up the fight it's not yours; don't give up the battle for the victory you will win will always be yours. If you just turn it over to Jesus I say to all women, and know that He can God can and have it all in His hands.

Chronicles 29:11
Thine, O Lord, is the greatness, and the power, and the glory, and the victory, and the majesty; for all that is in the heaven and in the earth is thine; thine is the kingdom, O Lord, and thou art exalted as head above all.
Psalms 4:1

Hear Me when I call, O God of my righteousness;
thou hast enlarged me when I was in distress;
have mercy upon me, and hear my prayer.
Psalms 9: 1-3
I will praise thee, O Lord, with my whole heart; I will show forth all thy marvelous works. I will be glad and rejoice in thee; I will sing praise to thy name, O thou most High. When mine enemies are turned back, they shall fall and perish at thy presence.
Psalms 31:1
In You, O Lord, do I put my trust and seek refuge; let me never be put to shame or have my hope in You disappointed; deliver me in Your righteousness.

gCWWSIP

God's Christian Working Woman Still In Progress

Come, let's go on, women. Let's show the world that we stand up and are bold and proud and know that God is on our side. Even in our imperfection, God still loves us. Even though we have been lost and feel that we can't be found, God will pick us up, dust us off, and show us Grace and Mercy, and put us on the right path that we must go. Oh no more fight. Stop, women, and just pray and give it all to God the Father and step back and let him fight for you. While you just pray, turn your face to the wall and say NO MORE tears

fears

pain

suffering

loneliness

financial struggles

stress

hurt

insanity

torn or even scorned

Deliver me from the hurt and the pain, because I do not want to do this or have all these things that bind me. Take it all. I will not settle for this, but I will settle for you, God. I will call you and know that you are near me because I do trust you. I will trust you even if I have to walk this walk alone.
For God has made us women, and not we ourselves. Women, we will keep him in our hearts and in our minds, even when all the things around us go to the wayside and fade not to be anymore. Trust, women, and give it to God and watch all the pain and hurt go away.
I will not turn away. I am a woman who is God's work in progress, God's Christian working woman still in progress. I have come a long way, and I will work not to stray away and make it through all my days. Help me, Lord, and fix me, mold me, shield and protect me even if you have to protect me from myself. I will trust in you, Lord, every day, and I will trust that you will lead me through. Work on me, God. Help me, yes you and not just me, because I need you, and I do know that you will not fail me. So look out, world, for I am not the same that I use to be **now** you can see, and even if you can't or don't want to, I am God's Christian Working Woman Still in Progress. God made me, and **yes** He rules the world—yours and mine.

The Strength, Struggle and Power that God Gives

Strength, power, and struggle—these three words fit the path that I was looking for. Struggle when I thought that I could not make it day to day. God stepped in and made a way, and I had to struggle to make ends meet; I had to struggle to find out how to get a good job without depending on man. I had to make sure my kids ate a meal every day even if I did not, so I had to make sure that I found the means to provide and have day care for the children and a roof over our heads. I did not and needed not to depend on man to give me, take from me, or destroy me, and feel that he owned me.

Struggle, broken down to fit what it meant to me as I was going through my hard times. I knew I was not alone once I found my Lord and Savior Jesus Christ, so I use these letters to help me along the way.

S- Salvation, stand up and rise to the occasion to be strong in the Lord.

T- Time is all I had when I was waiting on the Lord to fix all my problems and my situation.

R- Relax, relate, and release, and see what the Lord has when you let go.

U- Ultimate price, I learned that when Jesus died for me he gave the most ultimate gift, laying down his life for us, and nothing can compare to that.

G- God gave us his son to carry our burdens, so why must I give up? Just give him my burdens, and he will fix them all.

G- Gift that Jesus gave was the best, and no one could compare to that. To me, Jesus laid down his life that I may have eternal life; this is the most precious gift, and to have that is more important than anything ever.

L- Love and life is when I came to the knowledge that Jesus could give that to me and would love me unconditionally. With all the flaws that I have and all the wrong doing that I did, He still loves me regardless of all my sins. I thought that I could get love from a man, but in the end man hurt me and let me down every time.

E- Everlasting. When I thought about it, tears fell down my face. Everlasting is something that never dies; that is what I was looking for as a broken, battered, beaten, woman—a woman scorned who needed to be healed. His love is everlasting to all men and women, so it's your for the asking. Step out and grab hold of it and never let go. It is us who let go and not the Lord.

Hold on, women. God has a ram in the bush for you, and you deserve all that He has for you. Never give up even when it has hurt you to the point where it feels like you can't return. Get up and dust yourself off and walk into the light.

Scorned, but not broken is what I said to myself, and as I came closer to the Lord and let him in, the scars started to become things of the past. Healing is what I needed to make it through, so I embraced the Lord with what I had left, and never let Him go.

I was happy to know that all I needed now was that man who sat high and looked low and never gave up on me.

Psalm
This poor man cried, and the Lord heard him,
and saved him out of all his troubles
Psalm 34:6
O taste and see that the Lord is good: blessed
is the man that trusteth in him
Psalm 34:8
Let thy mercy, O Lord, be upon us, according as we hope in thee
Psalm 33:22
The Lord is their strength, and he is the
saving strength of his anointed
Save thy people, and bless thine inheritance:
feed them also, and lift them up for ever
Psalm 28: 8-9

The Lord helps me in all that I do and gives me the strength to go on day by day. I will give all that I have because it belongs to you. I am a woman who has been through many trials and tribulations in my life and know that as I live, I will continue to keep going. Lord, if you hear me, I know you will help me and give me the strength not to lean on man, but to learn to lean on you. Help me to understand that if I feel like I am falling, I may be able to lean and fall into your arms, knowing that I am safe from all danger and harm. Let me know that if I lean on you, you can hold me up and give me the strength to go through whatever lies ahead.

> Lord, if I fall on my knees, let me fall so that I may give you all of me; and when I rise, I know that I have left it there never to pick it up again. I will trust in you to see me through the dark and dreary seas. Give me the smile, comfort, and the knowledge to understand that you don't make mistakes and it is all in your control. I will cease and halt, and I will sing praises unto thy name. I want to dwell in the most high place, and if the pains of affliction should come upon me, let

me be able to let you fill my mouth with prayer because I know you hear me and will help me make it through.

Psalm 92:1
It is a good thing to give thanks unto the Lord, and to sing praises unto thy name, O most High

Now, thank you, Lord, for the strength that you have given me this day. Knowing that I can do all things through Christ who gives me strength each and every day will truly help me to succeed in my daily walk as I journey along my way. Guide me, lead me, and talk to me, for I do not and will not understand what may come my way; but teach me, lead me, and help me to live, learn, and endure what lies ahead. For the Lord is my Shepherd, and I shall not want.

Amen

* * * *

Through the Eyes of a Woman Who Made it Through

I wonder why it is that you go to church and trust in the pastor to preach and teach to your soul so that you may get fed a great word and be blessed. I needed someone who I can trust and seek wisdom from as I was going through dealing with the minister who I was dating and I needed some Christian advice. So I went to one of my close minister friends who I have known for over six years and trusted him so I thought I could always go to him with all my concerns, and at the age of forty-three add a half I needed some advice. You put your all into believing that this man of God received a word from God and you must hear what is being said.

All that I know, all that has been instilled in me, I lost when I truly put my trust in a man of God. I have been touched in a way that only a man who God put in your life to be your husband should touch you.

A pastor, preacher, teacher, husband, and father did the unspeakable to a vulnerable woman. To take oneself out of the will of God just to seek one's pleasure and go where he should not have ever been is beyond me. I thought that while I was going through a hard time with the man that I loved, that I would go and receive some counseling from a pastor that I knew very well and trusted. But it hurt me spiritually and emotionally even more.

He did things to me that I thought a man in his status should not do, and it did not matter if he was married or not. You don't put your hands on my private area and tell me I will help you if you let me have sex with you, if you let me touch you and see what you taste like. I have wanted you and it does not matter if I am with someone no one will know if you don't tell, and then you can get what you need. I trusted him and confided in him, only to be messed up with thoughts running through my head and thoughts of fear. I ran out of the building never to show my face in this place this place where I am supposed to come for peace, "I will no longer trust a pastor," is what I told myself. But I had to come to the realization that every pastor is not chosen, and you will have to ask God to show you the right way and put all your hurts, wants, needs, and troubles in him, and the Lord will lead and guide you to right way and you will be safe.

Jesus will walk with me and talk with me because I am tired of going through this torment and my mind needs to be at ease. *Help me, God,* I cried, lying awake at night. *What I can do when I just want to give it all up?* I do not have any trust right now in any man. For as we know that the Bible says not to put all your trust in any man because they will let you down every time. Even trusting a man of the cloth because they also are human and they fall regardless of the title that they hold, for they can be clothed as sheep in wolves clothing. My circle is very small and few, so now all I have to do from this day forth is call on the Lord. Yes, he will see me through. Trust and believe because Jesus will never let you down.

Living for a purpose

I have come to the knowledge that God is the head and that I can do all things through Christ who gives me strength. Even though I have been through the wilderness and the storms, the clouds were dark, and it seemed as though they were always surrounding me, raining on me with many showers of unforgettable hurt and pain. I have made it through for his purpose, and God will use me if I so desire to let him be my head.

Though it seems sometimes that depression weighed me down and the tears flowed as a river down my face, I understand now that God is able. Although it felt that I was always all alone, I have come to realize that God has been and will always be there for me no matter what time of day, the minute, even the hour that I call on him. He has and will always be there for me. Though the storms will always rage in my life and family may fall by the wayside and even the friends that I thought were there leave, God sees all that I am going through knows and feel and wants me to seek him and call on him. He won't leave you nor will He forsake you. Even when you feel that you are all alone, just call Him, and He will be right there, and all your worries will be gone if you let Him work and work alone.

God's grace and mercy has brought me and has carried me

all this way, and I have put all my trust in Him, and I will stand tall for living for a purpose. I will trust now in the Lord with all my heart, mind, and soul. I have walked through a dark tunnel, and yes I will come out as pure gold. To God be the glory, I made it, and you, too, can make it by being a strong woman of God. Even though you have been pushed in a corner, you have been beaten, you have been ridiculed, and lied to, know that you are one of a kind.

A woman who has been torn down, stepped on, rejected, and unloved is who I was, and no longer will you ever take me through and tear me up and turn out to be just like you. I have a purpose for you, and I need you to carry on and know that I will help you if you rely on me. I heard Jesus say, "Even when the times get hard and you just want to fall, let me take you through so that what I need you to do you can complete." Be strong proud hold your head up high; you are a child of God—happy and educated, full of joy, love, and much peace.

The Untold Secret

Have you ever been given some news that would take a tremendous toll on your life and alter your course? Some things should be left uncovered, and some things should have been uncovered a long time ago. The news that rocked my world took me by surprise and had me take a long look at why I was treated the way that I was growing up, and how it possibly had a great effect on my life, as well.

My mother took a great secret to her grave, and after forty-three years I found out.

Secrets. What do they really mean and why do we hold them for such a long time? Is it to help someone so that they won't be hurt or is it to make their life a living hell? Sometimes we love secrets because when revealed it may be a surprise for something special coming up, but sometimes it is a surprise that some may not want you to find out. My secret started like this.

I used to say to my mother growing up that I was adopted because of the way she treated me and the differences she made between my sister and me. The comparison she would bring up between the two of us always stayed in my mind from then to now. How pretty she is, and she will grow up to be the wonderful model, how she looks when she fixed up her face and how skinny she is. I once never heard that from my mother when all I received from her out of her own mouth was that she wished she never had me.

I would always have questions and go to different aunts and one of my uncles and ask why my mother treated me so wrong. I would always get the response that I shouldn't worry. I do know growing up I started rebelling against my mother because of how I was being treated.

When my mom died, my grandmother told me in her room at my aunt's house, "I just wish that before your mother died, she would have told you something." When I went to visit my grandmother down in the country, she brought this same statement back to me and said, "I wish your mother had told you something that is hurting me, and I just can't tell you because it would hurt. I want to tell you something, but I just can't because it would kill me." I said, "What is it? Tell me why you won't. I will be okay. You can tell me, and I won't tell anyone." She said, "One of your aunts will have to tell you. I just don't know how, and I won't be around long, and I wish I could but maybe one day somebody will tell you."

Years and months went by, and my big momma died, and mentioned what she said to my uncle and one of my aunts, but I never heard a word from anyone. I decided to go to visit my aunt out of the blue; she has helped me out along the way. My relationship with her was that I could always come to her no matter what and she would love on me and do for me when I needed her the most; although she would say things to make me cry, I still loved her in spite of it all. She helped me when my babies were small and I needed her, and she was there with no hesitation or bad word from her lips.

As I entered into her home, I greeted her and then sat down at the table. I had my grandchildren with me—my son's two babies—because I wanted them to see the children. So as they played with my cousin's children, I was talking to my aunt about some things that were on my mind and started to mention what Big Momma had said. I asked my aunt why my momma treated me so bad and why my sister was her favorite. As we were getting deeper into the conversation, I said, "I just don't feel the love and don't understand why I went through being treated that way?" My cousin came into the room and said, "I am tired. Enough is enough. She needs to know the truth."

My cousin said to me, "You know the reason why you feel that way because it is somewhat true. Your daddy that you think is your daddy is not your daddy. I know who your daddy is, and you need to talk to our cousin in Jefferson, Texas. She can help you to understand." I said, "What? This can't be true."

She was saying my daddy who raised me was not my daddy. He was my sister's, but not mine. My mom got pregnant while she was in the twelfth grade, and my big momma did not want her and my father together. My cousin said that she didn't know the whole story, but used to hear them talk about it a lot. She told me my real dad came to Fort Worth when I was a little girl to see me several times, but my mom would not let him see me. One time she said he came, and we were playing and he saw me, but my mom caused a big commotion, and he had to leave. He also was at the funeral, and they kept him away from me so I would not find out then.

Why did my father who raised me not tell me? He could have taken the time to sit me down and explain to me the truth about my life. What were his excuses for covering up what was supposed to be opened and revealed?

I was told to call my cousin, so I did. She clarified some things, and it was something that was told to me with the entire story at hand. She was around my mother's age and they attended school together and the word was out at that time around the school. She knew my dad and knew they were dating at that time. She told me that they were to get married, but our big momma sent my mother away.

She said, "I thought your mom told you. We thought you knew, because she said she would wait and tell you when it was time to do so." I started crying, and she said, "Don't cry, I will give you the phone number to your dad. Let me call some classmates, and I promise I will help you find your dad."

As the hours and just a couple of days went by, the thoughts that were flowing in my head seemed to rush like a river on a stormy day. I started wondering why my momma did this to me. My heart was filled with pain, and my mind was filled with bad thoughts. I wished she was here so I could tell her how I really felt and what she had done to me. *Who am I really?* I said to myself. *What does this man who is my real father look like? Do I look like him?* I always used to say to my mom and my sister that we didn't look alike.

When I meet this man who is my father, what should I say or how should I react? Does he think that now I may want something from him?

The tears that flowed down my face and the pain that I was feeling I cannot even describe. My God, I see now that everything can't be revealed at one time, because if it does I would not be able to handle it. God, what is to come before me? When do I finally get to see this man who is my father? Why did he not try harder to fight to see me? What was it really about? You will have to be with me through it all because I can't handle this one. It is too big for little me—the one who has been through it all.

I am so glad that I am in church, I said to myself and that I know a man who sits high and looks low, and he will be there to see me through all of this. My God can and will handle this. He has been by my side, and He has never left me alone. My God has been walking with me and talking to me since I gave my life and soul to Him. I heard God say to me, *Child just let me take it and give it all to me and you will be okay.* All the heartache and all the pain I felt started subsiding along with the tears when I asked God to help me through this and make the hatred become feelings of forgiveness and love regardless of what I was about to go through. I had been lied to by men and also friends who

I thought were there for me, but to be betrayed and hurt by my mom was worse.

I began to sing a song to ease my mind so that I would be able to sleep. God, just wrap your loving arms around me and give me comfort or peace. Give me wisdom; ease my mind, and give me peace that passes all understanding. As I fell asleep, I sang these words that would help me:

I've learned how to live holy and I have learned how to live right.

I've learned how to suffer, for if I suffer I know I will gain eternal life.

God, help me to forgive when the time comes. Let not the wrong words come out of my mouth that it may do more harm than good. Be there and guide me. Let me lean on you, for you are all I need in this time that I may call trouble.

So much trouble in my way, I have to cry sometimes. So much trouble I have to cry sometimes. I lie awake at night, but that's all right because I know Jesus will fix it after a while.

I received the phone call from my cousin, and she gave me a number to call my father, and told me who to ask for. I said, "Who is this?" She said, "This is one of your aunts, your dad's sister." So I called him and introduced myself to her and her as well to me. We spoke and she told me some things and asked me questions. She said she would contact my father and have him to call me. Oh how happy that turned out to be.

While waiting for the phone call that would change my life completely, I received a phone call from a young lady who introduced herself to me as my cousin, my aunt's daughter, whom I had just spoken with. We spoke and got to know each other and ended up meeting each other.

Thank you, God, for this opportunity and for opening up the closed doors in my life that I may now fully come to the knowledge of some things in my life. He said, *I will open doors that man thought they closed.*

When Daddy Calls

As the days went by, I was thinking that I would never hear from the man that I knew as my biological dad. I went to work as usual, going about my busy schedule but feeling like something was going to happen on this particular day. I felt nervous inside, and different thoughts were running through my mind. I previously spoke to my children and laid everything on the table that I was told about my father who raised me and my biological father who I was just introduced to. Hearing what I had encountered and how well I digested what was presented to me, was hard. It felt like I was taking a pill with no water.

My kids all have a voice of their own and gave me their opinion. I knew something was going to happen on this day, because I had an uneasy feeling in the pit of my stomach, but I anticipated something that I thought was a feeling about my oldest son.

I had just put a patient into a room where I was working so that the doctor could see about the patient's needs, and I received a phone call. The voice that I heard on the other end was not a voice that I recognized; it was a voice that was quite pleasant to hear. The man on the other end said, "Hello, this is your daddy." I was so overwhelmed with hearing him, and I just broke down and cried. The man who called himself my dad said to me in a sweet, kind voice, "Don't cry," and that he would like to speak with and see me.

"All I want is to see you," I said to him. "To talk to you, and at any time you decide not to do so and want to quit I want have no remorse. I know that I did just what I was supposed to do and that was to find my dad." He stated to me in a clear voice, "I would love to see you, as I have all my life been trying too, so we will meet, sit down, and talk."

The phone call that I received as I hung the phone up changed my entire life from then on. The tears that flowed down my face were now tears of joy. After all this time I had a father who I had never seen and who would like to get to know me. I also from that small conversation found out I was the firstborn of six children, whom I may seek the opportunity one day to see.

We talked for just a brief moment, but it was so sweet to know that what was done and hid away never to be revealed was brought out for the best part in my life. God has a way of bringing out what he needs to at his own time.

There is a time and a season for everything, and it is not our will but the will of our precious Jesus who will always show up and show us things that we need to know whether bad or good. To God I do give all the honor and praise because it is through Him I too will make it through this journey that lies ahead for me. The Lord my God sits high and looks low, sees all, and knows all I said to this man, so when I meet you I will truly know if you are really my biological dad. He said to me, "There is no doubt in my mind. I have been there all the time, but I just was not given the opportunity to be the man whom you were to call dad."

Before we hung up, this man said to me, "I will not say goodbye. I will say later, because when you say goodbye you are saying goodbye to someone you will never see again, and I plan on meeting you." So I took all he said and stored it in my head so that I might go and pray and ask God to help me. I gathered my thoughts and said yes to him I won't say goodbye either I will say later. The word later it will be.

Revelation 3:8

God closes doors no man can open, and God opens doors no man can close.

When God leads you to the edge of the cliff, trust Him fully and let go. Believe that He can and He will do one of two things: either He'll catch you when you fall or He'll teach you how to fly. You never know who God will send to help you open that door, so trust in Him to see you through all the way. Let go and let God. Be blessed in all that you do each and every day, and remember to be a blessing to everybody.

The Day that I Met My Natural Father

As the days and weeks went by, I spoke to my biological father almost every day. He told me the story about how he met my mom, and how I came to be, and what happened with them. He said he planned to marry my mom, but on the day they were supposed to wed, he went to the court house, but she was not there. So he went to my big momma's house, but my mom was nowhere to be found. He told me that he saw my mom sitting in a car as it passed by with a man who would later turn out to be my step-father, and the look on her face was priceless as if she wanted him to come and save her. But my dad did nothing because he was confused at what was going on and what he was seeing, because he knew that my mom and he would be together. My biological dad knew she was pregnant with me, because at their high school graduation, they marched down the aisle together rubbing her belly. In the end it was discovered that Big Momma had a lot to do with my mom leaving to be with my step-father who was my step-father the one true man that raised me.

My real dad's family did know about me, and he even had a sister who saw me a lot because my mom kept in contact with her, although at the time I knew her only as my mom's best friend. My dad and I decided to meet for the first time. It happened to be his birthday. I, and the gentleman I was dating at the time, met my father and his wife after church to spend father and daughter time together for the first time ever. I was 43 years old.

I was feeling so nervous, not knowing what to expect. I wondered how he would feel when he saw me for the first time. That Sunday, the moment that I had anticipated was drawing so close as we entered into the restaurant. My heart was pounding, and it felt as if the walls were closing in on me and I was smothering. My hands were sweating as I held onto the gift that I picked out for my dad, almost crumpling the bag with intense shaking in my knee. These were the feeling I felt that lead up to the meeting of my biological father.

Time was ticking, and every time a man entered the restaurant, I wondered, "Is that my daddy?" Then, a man and a young lady approached us, and I looked at the man and started to break down and cry, because it looked like I was looking in a mirror. I knew without a shadow of doubt that it was my father. "Oh daddy," I said, with tears of joy running down my face. He just hugged me and started crying, "My baby, my baby, I had always waited for this moment, my baby." We forgot that we were holding up the line, but no one even said a word.

We went through the line with tears of joy running down our faces and the excitement of finally being able to fill the void that was once empty. We sat down and shared pictures and the events that had happened in our lives. Knowing my true family history was quite exciting, and seeing actual pictures of my siblings filled my heart. The exchange of the gift which was a bottle of expensive cologne was so sweet, and my dad told me later he would cherish it for a lifetime because it came from me.

I told my dad he had grandchildren and great-grandchildren and showed photos of them, and I watched his eyes widen as he viewed the photos with tears.

I sat in his lap and he held me although I am a grown woman now my dad just wanted to hold me he said, saying "I never got to hold my daughter nor see her grow up, but I thank God that he has allowed us to enjoy what we have for the future."

He came to my house, and we sat and talked some more, what a wonderful time we were having laughing and talking about how our lives had been so far and how it will be as we enter into a new journey as a family. Then we embraced each other, and I told him, "This will not be the last time we meet and greet one another." So my dad and his wife left, and I watched with tears flowing down my face. We did not say goodbye, we said later. My dad says saying *goodbye* means not seeing each other again, so *later* is our word.

A Love I Once Had

(What a man once said to me)

I remember a love I once heard a man say to me. He thought that I would always be there; even through all the hurt and abuse that he placed upon me. He thought I would never leave. The truth came to face him, and he said, "As I lay with very strong thoughts of you in my head, I started to feel sad as I thought of the woman I thought I had."

For a great woman, I once loved and did wrong, and I just knew I had her for the long haul my husband said to me. I would remember to myself back on how strong our love used to be when we were so in love my second husband and me. I thought to myself, in love with a man who would ridicule and yes tried his best to even beat on me. I never thought I would be in this place so hurt and full of pain and misery, but I truly now live in a place where I can truly be free from all hurt, harm and shame.

Cover me even from myself so I will not be hurt again from the love I once had; please take the tears and the pain away so the sun can shine on a new day and not the rain. It wasn't you that broke us up he said to me from behind a window pane locked secured from hurting me; it was mostly me, he would say as he wished he could get down on one knee to express deeply how he did me. I am not the man I truly need to be, and know I pushed you to a point of no return you will never ever belong to me. No matter what I do to try to please you I will never have you back and now I'm hurting too. Thinking back to how it was at one time, I will leave this way knowing that you will always be mine; no matter how many women I've had, you were and will always be mine till the end.

I have been around and seen a lot of things and treated women like I did, so when I receive a great gift from above, I did not know how to treat the angel God gave to me no I did not even have a clue. He told me when I think of you, I get a very big lift, as you made me smile; even when I was not being the man I should have been to you and stood by your side.

Remembering that I was given one of God's greatest gifts, that gift was you, more precious than having an Armani suit. I love so, dear Tonya I loved you with all my heart now we are apart. I've loved many women and the intimacy with them was not quite the same as it was with you, so I will put your mind at rest; your love was always the same, and yes it was all so true the love you gave I hold to be true.

Once not long ago, someone told me to stay with you Tonya he said to me, and that was a true friend indeed and I did not realize what he was telling me until our relationship came to a complete end now I am here begging on my knees. Now I know quickly and abrupt never to see you once again I lost my good friend. I miss your love so as I sit here dreaming of what was once and now never will be. Sadness rose deep within me I would run to you if only you would take me back with no hesitation and give you all that I own the love I once had. So remember and please forgive me because I was the one you once loved you were the angel that heaven sent to me from above.

So Glad I Made It

Through all my heartaches, my pains, my ups and downs, I made it. If you walk by me and see me cry, don't worry. I'm just going through what God is allowing me to go through so that I may fulfill the plan he has for me. Yes, I may not see it and don't really know why, but I heard Him say, *It is for your good, so walk through it although it may hurt. Call me, and I will guide you through it until you reach safety.*

Although it may seem like I lost everything, I did not lose my faith; so yes I have to keep moving forward so that my testimony can be spoken to help all other women get through that fiery storm and be strong. And at the end, through all the scars, through all the pain, through all the mental and physical abuse, and knowing that I could have lost my mind, I say I made it through and I am still alive to be here to see me and to see you. God has a plan for me, and it is working for my good so that he can use me to benefit for his glory that others who are and will be going through see and know He has you the whole time in the palm of his hands and can see you through.

Hold on in spite of all; hold on and hold your head up high and be strong and know you are still alive to declare that you never lost your faith in Jesus and say in the end, I'm so glad I made it through.

I made it through.....................................
I made it through
Pain, abuse
loneliness, hurt, calamity,
homeless, struggle, rape,
surgeries, heartaches

Shoes

The shoes that I walked in and the shoes that were meant for me daily are the shoes that were filled for me. My shoes were only meant for me and me alone, and no one could take over and replace what was designed just for me. These shoes may have been small in size, but they were great in different aspects of life. Sometimes these shoes were high, sometimes the shoes were low, and many times wide; but through wearing them, I kept hold and kept them on and walked in them as I needed to. Sometimes my toes hung out over the edge and the heals were rough and tough, and everything I did to make my feet look good in the shoes did not work, because it was me trying instead of giving it over to someone who could help. Sometimes the soles of the shoes were worn down to nothing and the holes were so big that all I could do was my best to keep them on and walk forward in what was prepared for me.

Romans 10:15 And how shall they preach, except they be sent? As it is written, how beautiful are the feet of them that preach the gospel of peace, and bring glad tidings of good things!

Shoes, oh shoes, you got so tight to me that I even tried many times to take them off and throw them away. Then I would have been all alone. In spite of the journey, I made it through all obstacles that were placed in front of me. See, not everyone can wear your shoes, because they were meant for the individual, designed and placed on the proper person and given a certain task. Though they may take you on a path, through the mud, the slime, the filth, the dirtiness, and the water, you will make it through. Hills I will climb up, and valleys I will have to endure and walk through, waddling my way through just to fulfill the race that was placed before me. I can and will, with these shoes, make it through.

God planned for me to wear these shoes, and I will do as he permits me to do so. I prepare on a daily basis to put them on and ask God for the understanding and the knowledge to prepare my mind and heart to make it through this journey. For as these shoes are placed on my feet, I will wear them with pride and hold my head high, for there is a man who sits high and looks low, who will guide me all the way through life's struggles and trials.

Shoes, let us take this walk now and go through what was meant for us to go through, and run this race until the sweet bitter end. And as I looked at these shoes, even though the shoes are sad, filthy, hurt, and even unclean from the many walks that were chosen for us, the feet are still beautiful and clean no matter what we go through. What was designed for you is for you, and only you. The chosen shoe was yours all along, and you have to step in and walk, having God by your side.

End of a Chapter

I have gone through so many different stages, changing ideas and goals while searching for the right kind of life for me. Lord, you were always ready to help me at all times, and it must have seemed like I would never follow one straight path. Now that I know what I am doing, I can only show you my extreme appreciation for your support by being true to all the ideas and values that you tried to teach me.

Thank you forever for standing by me. I love you and appreciate you forever. I want you to know that even though my feelings somehow don't get spoken like they should, the feelings are always warmly here in my heart for you.

And I would love to thank you for everything you are to me forever and all the wonderful things you continue to do.

Love cannot be touched or captured, locked up, or hoarded and saved. Love must be shown at all times until it dies, saying until you are gone on home. Love is pure, selfless, and everlasting. Love is timeless, transcending all barriers, touching the untold years. Love does indeed conquer all, and to be in love is to live happily ever after.

I wish there were a way to repay you for all that you've done for me, all the caring, all the love and the concern you had, and most of all, the sacrifice you bore on that rugged cross. I always know you will be there for me and that you never dwelled on what I did or said. You encouraged me to press forward for the higher mark and look toward the hills where my health comes from and reach my goals.

You taught me that mistakes don't mean failure, but that I need to try harder and succeed in life no matter what lies ahead for me, whether it is big or even small. So thank you for all the things you have done and for everything that made my being with you a very special time.

You are the best man that I have ever known who has not led me astray and not given up on me no matter how hard my life may have been. The qualities have made a lasting impression on me that I will admire for as long as I live. You give me so much to be thankful for and the great words-a sweetness that goes beyond. Most of all you taught me to dream with the universe as my boundaries and to reach for my goals that I must explore and go beyond the skies as far as my life, and yes the end of a chapter with a great beginning to a new life. A great life, as I am held in the arms of a loving God.

Places in God where he covers me, yes, and a place where we all can go and be free. Peace, love, joy is in this place-a great place where women like me can be free. I have been in a lot of places, but this is an amazing place to be. In the arms of Jesus is truly where I want to be. Love to all, and to God is the glory for all he has done, yes for you and, of course, even for me. Pray and live for Jesus. He will take care of you and all you need if you only give it to him. Love to my entire family. Let the sun shine and no more rain, we say, because Jesus is the reason why we celebrate in all seasons. Love mom, daughter, sister, and friends. My tears are going away, and I have seen a brighter day. Oh yes, Lord, my father is within you a place where I am truly **Free**.

Not an end of my life, and yes the end of a chapter that scorned me but never to return to that life again. I have a great beginning to a new life, a great life as I am held in the arms of a loving God. I am truly **Free**.

To my dad, **Verdale "Von" Denis McCray**, a man does not have to conceive a baby to take of a baby that is not biologically his own. But it takes a real man who you are to take on a great responsibility of caring for and loving the child as your very own.

You taught me in time to build up the strength to prove to myself that I am able to be the woman God wanted me to be. You taught me through the words that came from your very lips to stand up and fight for myself when I am torn down. That is what came to my mind as the years went by.

Words hurt and I had to allow God to shield me and make me strong through words.

I know now through your **love** now you are really proud of me because as time came, went and gone you now verbally say it and I give all praise to God through many prayers over the years.

To forgive and move on and show love daily is what I have in my heart for you daddy.

Thank you for all you have done for me, because now I know time helps all scars and wounds to heal, and I do so love you from the bottom of my heart.

Love your daughter always,
Tonya Michelle Ward-Blackshear

www.ingramcontent.com/pod-product-compliance
Lightning Source LLC
Chambersburg PA
CBHW071609080526
44588CB00010B/1077